LEAP

LEAP

Leaving a Job with No Plan B
to Find the Career and Life You
Really Want

TESS VIGELAND

HARMONY
BOOKS · NEW YORK

Published in the United States by Harmony Books, an imprint of the
Crown Publishing Group, a division of Penguin Random House LLC,
New York. www.crownpublishing.com

Harmony Books is a registered trademark, and the Circle colophon
is a trademark of Penguin Random House LLC.

Library of Congress Cataloging-in-Publication Data
Vigeland, Tess.
   Leap : leaving a job with no Plan B to find the career and life you
really want / Tess Vigeland.
       pages cm
   1. Career changes. 2. Career development. 3. Success in
business. I. Title.
   HF5384.V54 2015
   650.14—dc23
                                    2015009114

ISBN 978-0-8041-4075-1
eBook ISBN 978-0-8041-4076-8

Printed in the United States of America

Book design: Debbie Glasserman
Jacket design: Jess Morphew

10 9 8 7 6 5 4 3 2 1

First Edition

For my parents, Ted and Julie,
who never believed I was anything less
than remarkable

CONTENTS

LEAP

AUTHOR'S NOTE

Welcome, reader! That's a funny thing for me to write because I'm so used to saying, "Welcome, listener!" I imagine there are all kinds of reasons why you might be here. Some of you are probably my fellow leapers, my quitters-in-arms, those of you who have opted out from the path you were on and are heading off for uncharted territory. I'm so glad you're here, and you are the major inspiration for this book. I heard from thousands of you from across the globe as I was writing this book, and as much as it meant to *you* to know that you were not alone in your roller-coaster ride, it meant even more to me to know that *I* was not alone. You shared your stories with me and kept me updated for the better part of two years, and I loved it. I hope this book will provide comfort and insight for you as you figure out where to find your personal tub of kittens.

Welcome, too, to the public broadcasting faithful—the radio junkies among you. Maybe you're here because you wanted to hear my voice again, and I hope you do in these pages. You are why I loved my job for more than twenty years. You're the ones who know how to pronounce my name and can recognize me by voice when I'm talking with a friend in an elevator. Thank you for coming here, to the book page, where there is no sound but, I hope, there is still me.

And for those of you who didn't leap from your jobs or careers but instead were pushed? I hope you find some direction and solace here. There are, of course, major differences between quitting and being laid off or fired, not the least of which is that one is voluntary and the other is decidedly involuntary. I spoke with several people who had lost their jobs unexpectedly, people who did not have a plan B, and their emotional journey often included anger, humiliation, shame, and panic to an extent that we leapers usually do not experience. Those who were laid off or fired were also feeling enormous, sudden, and constant pressure to find a solution—a new job or a new career—immediately. They did not feel that they could take the time to reevaluate priorities, needs, and wants in the way that many quitters, including me, tend to (rightly) indulge.

But if it takes some time to find the next opportunity after a layoff—and more often than not in a post-meltdown economy, it does—you will probably find yourself asking some of the same questions and going through the same mental processes that we leapers do. I hope you will find the chronicling useful.

And welcome to those of you who picked up this book because you're thinking about making a change in your life. Perhaps a friend or a colleague at work suggested it. No matter what potentially life-changing transition you're considering or experiencing, I hope that this book gives you a new perspective on what you're going through. This is the story of what happens when you leap before you look—when you leave something major in your life without a plan and without knowing what you want to do next.

I look back on the two years between when I gave notice and when I finished this book, and I marvel at what has happened in my life. Those two years changed me, for the better I think, and what I will share with you here are the processes, the learning, the pain, the victories, and the defeats. I won't pretend that the lessons I've learned are necessarily applicable to everyone. But what I have discovered, in talking with so many others who leaped from their careers, is that there are commonalities in the experiences, in the crises and in the recoveries. These similarities create empathy among the members of this particular tribe. In almost every conversation I have had with the people you'll meet in these pages, there was at least one moment, usually more than one, when one of us would exclaim, "Exactly! You understand!" The relief in that moment was palpable.

The real people I feature in this book all quit their jobs without having anything else lined up. All of them shared their reasons for leaving their jobs, but understandably, they didn't want those stories shared publicly because they didn't want to burn any bridges. I respect that, and for that same reason, I have withheld the specifics of my own departure. I don't think those reasons are what's most important, or interesting, about what followed. There's that saying about how life is a journey, not a destination. I'd add that it's also not about the point of departure.

So within these pages you will not find "Ten Steps to Quitting Your Job." That's not what this is about. What I can promise you is a number of stories about people who risked everything but do not regret the journey they went on after leaping.

This is a story about coming to grips with the idea that you don't have to be defined by your work. This is also a reality check. Leaping is difficult. We are all expected to have five-year and ten-year plans. We are expected to have a dream of that next thing we want to do. But a lot of us don't. What we have is a fear of the unknown future and a severe allergy to sharing that fear with other people.

This is my inoculation against that allergy. Thank you for being here. Shall we hold hands as we leap?

PROLOGUE

Speech to the World Domination Summit (WDS) in Portland, Oregon, Sunday, July 7, 2013, Arlene Schnitzer Concert Hall

How many of you listen to public radio? How many of you listen to *Marketplace*? (I have tote bags for all of you backstage.) How many of you are fans of *This American Life*? OK, good. Well, I'm going to steal liberally today from how they construct their show each week. Of course, it also means I'm stealing liberally from every playwright ... ever. My life: in three acts. Here we go.

Act 1. I Always Knew What I Wanted to Do— or Pretty Close to That

So here's the one reaction I remember most from the day *Marketplace* announced I was leaving. It was the middle of August 2012. The press release went out on a Friday, and within minutes my inbox had flooded, the phone messages had piled up, and my Facebook page had lit up ... and this is the one little slice of communication I remember most. Six words:

WHAT THE HELL ARE YOU DOING?!?!?

Here it is again in case you didn't get that:

WHAT THE HELL ARE YOU DOING?!?!?

Six little words. About thirty characters. And I know that because it was a tweet. From an old high school friend. A wordsmith, clearly! No, really—he's one of the smartest people I know—and a better writer than I'll ever be. And no one was more succinct. And no one was more incisive:

What. The Hell. Are you doing.

I'm here to try to explain what the hell I was doing. Leaving a dream job. My own national radio show. A place I'd wanted to work from the moment I left college. For those of you who may not be familiar with it, *Marketplace* is a trio of hugely respected programs with a combined audience of more than nine million people.

It covers business and economics. The show's been around since about 1990, and it has an incredibly loyal following—as I said, some nine million people listen to it each week.

This was a perch from which I interviewed politicians, authors, and celebrities. A job that allowed me to actually help hundreds of thousands of people with a difficult issue: money. A microphone through which I was allowed to say almost anything—short of an FCC violation. A coveted spot in the world of national news media. A modest measure of celebrity within the small niche that is public broadcasting. A very nice salary. The respect of strangers and of my peers. Seriously proud parents.

And I walked away.

What. The Hell. Are you doing.

I am what you might call an "accidental journalist." I had

every intention, actually, of being a concert pianist. Started when I was five, and I spent my early high school years thinking about whether I wanted to go to Oberlin or Juilliard. Then in my junior year, my English teacher said, "You know what? You should write for the school newspaper."

And that's how I fell in love with the news.

I went to journalism school in Chicago. Did internships at newspapers, TV stations, and radio stations. My first job out of college in 1990 was with Oregon Public Broadcasting—just up the road here in Portland. And the very first national story I ever sold was to *Marketplace.* A story about the first-ever Niketown. And right about then, I decided I wanted to work there someday. Might take me twenty to thirty years to get there, but I'd try.

It took eleven years. *Marketplace* called in mid-2001 and asked me to come host a show. Of *course,* I said yes.

The show was the *Marketplace Morning Report*—a series consisting of seven newscasts each hour starting at 2:50 a.m. Pacific time. Kai Ryssdal and I shared those duties for several years. He went on to host *Marketplace*—and he still does. In 2006 I became the host of *Marketplace Money,* our weekend personal finance program.

Now that you know I was in personal finance, let me quickly get this out of the way:

❚ Don't spend more than you earn.
❚ Contribute to your 401(k) at *least* to the match.
❚ Don't carry a balance on your credit card.
❚ Save for retirement before you save for the kids' college.
❚ Don't listen to the clowns on CNBC.

▌And, mamas, don't let your babies grow up to be cowboys unless they can find a good health plan!

Follow those and you'll be rich.

OK.

So I had this amazing job, right? Every week we produced this show where we took calls from people who had questions about money. We ran stories about everything from figuring out the cost of personal safety—my producer sent me to a gun range—to figuring out how to buy wine—my producer sent me to a wine store for that one, God bless his soul. I traveled the country to write about money for the *New York Times*. I took my microphone anywhere and everywhere that would have me. I got to visit places and people that few other people do.

I had fans. People who would recognize me in elevators just by my voice. Perfect strangers who thought I was awesome and had the coolest job in the world. Who wouldn't love that?!

And after eleven years of that, eleven years at *Marketplace*, I walked away.

What. The Hell. Are you doing.

Here's where I'm supposed to tell you that the reason I left is because I was restless. I wanted to do something different. I wanted to pursue another dream or passion. I wanted to see what else the world had to offer. I was happy and fulfilled and ready for a new challenge, right?

Well, part of that is true. I was restless. I wanted to do something different. But I never wanted to leave *Marketplace*.

Now, given that this is a public forum, I won't tell stories about my departure. I'll save that for my memoirs.

What I will say is that I had been unhappy for a while. I

was tired of the subject I had been covering week in and week out. There are about six stories in personal finance, and I had told them over and over and over again. I had gotten to the point where I wanted to reach through the radio, take listeners by the shoulders, and say, "Don't you get it? Don't spend more than you save! That's it! I told you this last week! And the week before that! Do I really I have to tell you again this week?" (I didn't do that, of course, because . . . physics.)

But in the end I left for a very personal reason. An unhappy one that culminated in an afternoon of heavy tears, after which I told my husband, "I'm sorry, but I'm done. I have to leave. I have to jump without a net." He said, "OK—we'll make it work."

One of the questions it was suggested I try to answer today is, How do you know when it's time to go? How do you know when to leap without a net?

And the answer in my case is that it's time to leave when you have too much self-respect to stay.

That, and when you're so stressed out you start losing your hair. True story. Pay attention if *that* happens.

Now please understand that I do not regret one second of my time at *Marketplace*. And maybe it was just time to go anyway. Eleven years is a good long while to be in one place. And I truly loved that place. I was meant to be there. And it helped me become the journalist—and the person—I am today.

But what you can probably gather now is that when I left, it wasn't for another dream. It wasn't something I had expected to do or that I had planned for months or years. I left a sure thing for the vast unknown. And it was easily the most terrifying thing I've ever done.

People kept saying, "Oh, Tess, this is so exciting for you!

You can do anything! You're so brave! You're doing what so many people would *love* to do! And by the way, you are famous, and people will walk through fire to work with you! Hey, you should give a speech about this to three thousand people in Portland!"

Yes! Fantastic! I am brave and awesome! I will go on to even bigger and better things!

Either that—or I'm the most insane fountain of idiocy on the planet.

What. The Hell. Are you doing.

Act 2. Whatdya Wanna Do Now, Punk?

What's amazing about a leap of faith is how everyone around you is so sure it's going to work out—when deep down you are so sure it won't. I think maybe they don't know what else to say. I mean, what, they're going to hear you're leaving your high-profile national broadcasting job with an economy barely in recovery from the worst recession in decades, and they're going to say, "Oh, no, don't do it. It will never work out, and hey, good luck with that though!"

No, of course not. What they will repeat over and over is how you're chasing the dream of every worker bee who's ever lived. And we know that's the case for most people, right? In fact, just recently Gallup released the results of its most recent employee engagement survey, reporting that out of the 100 million Americans with full-time jobs, 70 percent—repeat, 70 percent—are disengaged. The survey mentions how these disengaged people cost companies money as they "roam the halls spreading discontent."

So, yeah. At least I quit instead of roaming the halls spreading discontent. Yay me!

I had a big party the Saturday after my final day in the newsroom. Friends made speeches about how proud they were of me and how excited they were to see what I would be doing next—and all I could think was, What the hell am I going to do next?

Less than two weeks later, I had an answer. Guy Raz announced he was leaving as the host of NPR's *Weekend All Things Considered.* If you're not familiar with the show, that's a big deal. It's a big deal. Holy cow, this is what I'm going to do next! This was meant to be! But wait. Don't get ahead of yourself. Send in your résumé and contact a couple of the top leaders at NPR to let them know you're interested. Chill out because you're probably not going to get it.

But, jeez, the timing! Oh, and by the way, they're moving the show from DC to LA, where I live. It was meant to be!

We'll get back to *Weekend All Things Considered* in a bit—I'm going to give you a taste of just how long public radio takes to make hiring decisions.

Meanwhile all of these people were saying how great it was that I had given up my dream job for . . . a dream. But here's the thing. When you have your dream job, or something really, really close to it, you don't spend a lot of timing dreaming about what else you might want to do with your life. Why would you?

What everybody wanted to know was this: What was I going to do next? And I had the lamest answer of them all: "I don't know."

The follow-up question was even worse: Well, what did I *want* to do?

I wanted to go home and curl up with my cats.

"No, no, Tess. Go read *What Color Is Your Parachute?* Watch some TED talks about finding your passion. Go take a class that you've always wanted to take."

Great advice. But inside my head, I was paralyzed. Getting your brain to really, really open up to all the possibilities is so much harder than I ever imagined.

I know a lot of you here are entrepreneurs so maybe you were good at seeing possibilities—it wasn't a struggle for you. Starting a business is, of course, a struggle, but maybe your brain was quick to absorb the idea of trying something completely new.

Not mine. I did the same thing for a long time. And I got pretty close to the top of my field when I was thirty-two years old. So this question—for me—was a doozy.

But here's the thing: I think it's a doozy for a lot of us. In fact, I started to turn it around on my friends. And a lot of them didn't have an answer. So let me ask you:

Into audience
(Asking audience members: What do you do? Do you like it? If
you could quit today, what would you want to do?)
Back on stage

As the months went by, I kept trying to figure out an answer to this question because people kept asking it. And while I thought about it, I kept doing what I was good at. As a freelancer, I hosted a show called *America Abroad*, which was great because when I was doing interviews about terrorists in northern Mali, nobody was asking me about allocating their 401(k)s. I hosted several shows at the public radio stations in

Los Angeles, I did some freelance features for a few websites and broadcast outlets, and I wrote a long piece for the *New York Times.*

In February, NPR called me for a preliminary phone interview for that *Weekend All Things Considered* job. By then I had heard the job would be going to an internal candidate, so I didn't put much stock in the idea that I might get that job. You know—the one I was made for.

Meanwhile I was talking with people about producing podcasts, maybe going on a speaking tour with a friend of mine who's a former financial adviser. Another friend of mine and I came up with this idea for a reality TV show, and we actually got a meeting at a big agency in Hollywood: the Creative Artists Agency!

I really loved all these experiences and thinking about all these new things I could do with my life. They were exciting and different—and proof that there was life beyond public radio, proof that I had value beyond public radio.

Maybe I should do something totally different. Just go try something new.

Then in April, NPR called and wanted to know if I'd like to do an in-person interview for the *Weekend All Things Considered* job. Are you kidding me? Yeah. A couple of producers flew out from DC to LA to interview me, and I nailed it. You know how you just know when something important has gone well? Yeah, that's what I felt like when I left. But I was also still hearing—and you all know that reporters are just glorified gossips, right?—about a couple of other candidates who were shoe-ins. So the producers went back to DC, and I went back to freelancing and guest hosting shows.

But in the back of my head, I started to think, Well, maybe this could really happen. Is it really possible that I could be the next host of *Weekend All Things Considered*? And I can tell you that when that possibility starts invading your consciousness, good luck trying to think beyond it.

So this notion that, hey, I'll just go do something different, find another passion, that went away pretty quickly. Which was not wise—hope is a dangerous thing sometimes, but it's also a fun thing to have when you've got one eye on the future and one on the past, and you think they might just come together.

A week went by. Then two. Then three. And I'm thinking, OK, it's over.

And this, ladies and gentlemen, is what the last eight months or so were like. Something really cool would happen, and then, crickets.

Hosting *America Abroad* to great success: I AM AWESOME. I AM TALENTED. PEOPLE LOVE ME!

Next three weeks: WHAT HAVE I DONE? I WILL NEVER HAVE ANOTHER JOB AGAIN!

Hosting a show in LA for a week to great success: I AM AWESOME. I AM TALENTED. PEOPLE LOVE ME!

Next two weeks: WHAT HAVE I DONE? I WILL NEVER HAVE ANOTHER JOB AGAIN!

Big story in the *New York Times*—made the top ten most e-mailed list: I AM AWESOME. I AM TALENTED. PEOPLE LOVE ME!

Next day: WHAT HAVE I DONE?

Eight months on this roller coaster. Stop the world, I want to get off!

Then NPR asked if I'd like to come to DC and audition for *Weekend All Things Considered.* As in, Would I do the show? For an entire weekend. In Washington. One of 4 finalists— out of 160 candidates. Why, yes, I think that would be fine, thank you.

So about a month later, I spent a week at NPR's gleaming new headquarters.

And I had the Time. Of. My. Life.

Yes, being on *Marketplace* was a big deal—it's a huge show. But this was bigger. I did an interview with John Mellencamp, Stephen King, and T Bone Burnett *together.* Had one of the first on-air interviews with the reporter who broke the Snowden NSA spying story. Did this great piece about the National Aquarium in Baltimore. When I walked out of the studio on that Sunday, the staff stood and applauded me.

I could not have had more fun if I was bathing in a tub of kittens. *This* was what I was meant to do. *This* was why I had left a sure thing for the unknown. *This* was why I'd had such a tough time figuring out what else I wanted to do. Because this was the next step in my career and in my life.

The show's producer told me they got six times the number of listener feedback letters than they usually got—all positive. Unbeknownst to me, they also had a set of a hundred core listeners across the country evaluating me and my performance that weekend—a focus group. And *they* thought I was great. My parents, my friends, and perfect strangers said there was no way I wouldn't get that job. I'm pretty sure John Mellencamp would've said the same thing. It was meant to be.

I AM AWESOME. I AM TALENTED. PEOPLE LOVE ME!

So I got the call a little over a week ago.

And . . .

I will *not* be the next host of *Weekend All Things Considered.*

I placed second in the NPR host sweepstakes. Literally—
they told me I was the runner-up.

Whatdya wanna do now, punk?

Act 3. Getting Back to Remarkable

When J. D. Roth asked me earlier this year about speaking at
this event, I told him, "Well, you've got this theme about being
remarkable in a conventional world. And I'm not feeling very
remarkable anymore."

How can I pretend to tell anyone else how to be? Especially
when there are so many people here who've really thought
about that idea, who have some fantastic advice for you, things
for you to go out and do and try and act on—presentations
with bullet points and fun illustrations and real insight.

I don't have any of that. I'm a journalist. At least I think I
still am. For now. We're a generally cynical lot, not especially
given to real introspection or self-analysis. Or PowerPoints.

So—remarkable? I don't feel remarkable. At least not anymore.

I was, however. I think I was pretty remarkable for having
a career of more than two decades. I was lucky to strike gold
with the first job I got. Not everyone can say that their first gig
turned out to be the only thing they ever wanted to do.

I worked hard for it, but the journey itself wasn't really that
hard. I never struggled to get a job, and I never struggled to
keep a job. And in the end, hundreds of thousands of people,
on a good day more than a million, wanted to listen to me, to
what I had to say.

For eleven years I was "*Marketplace*'s Tess Vigeland." She and that were nothing short of remarkable.

Now I'm just—Tess Vigeland.

And I have to figure out how *she* is remarkable.

I know in my head that they're the same person. But will anyone want to listen to me if I'm not a national journalist anymore? What if I decide to follow what I think might be another passion and go work for the Red Cross, admirably, but relatively anonymously? Do I lose all my Twitter followers and all the fans—strangers—who've friended me on Facebook? Will I disappoint all those people who think I was really great at what I did? Does it matter? Why do I care what other people think? I *know* I'm not supposed to care, but I do.

How do I get back to remarkable?

The *only* way is by redefining it.

And I think this is an exercise that's going to take some time. We all know we're not supposed to define ourselves and our success by money, by page views, by Twitter followers, by fan mail, by audience size. But if you have a job, it does define you in many ways. You spend a good chunk of your day at that job—whether that's at home or in an office or out in the field. Your lifestyle is sometimes determined by how much that job compensates you. I'm on track right now to make one-third of what I made last year. One-third. I know that doesn't define me, but it does contribute to how I see my own value. I like what money allows me to do in my life.

So I need to redefine what success means to me. I don't know how to define that without an audience. I don't know how to define that without strangers' recognizing my voice in an elevator. If that sounds egotistical—well, you don't go into broadcasting without some amount of ego. It is a performance, after all. And if I end up doing something that can't or won't feed it, how do I know if I'm succeeding? How do I know if I'm remarkable?

Well, first of all, because the people who know me best—the people who love me—tell me I am. Even now. So I'm not going to call them liars.

Second of all, I'm remarkable because I *did* leave. I've got a set. I've got some Paddy Chayefsky in me after all.

And my life hardly fell apart. It's pretty good, in fact, when I stop and think about it. I'm still working. I've actually turned down opportunities over the last eight months because either they were in places I decided I didn't want to live or because they just didn't feel right. And I have to believe something really great is out there for me to find and catch.

Now, I know I'm supposed to tell you that this has all been a wonderful learning experience, that I'm a better person for the challenge, that I've grown, and that this was all really good for me.

Instead, I'll tell you it has been terrifying, it has been awful, and it has been heartbreaking.

It's made me doubt my decision-making ability. It's made me wonder if I'm in some loop of self-destruction. It's made me question whether everyone who's ever told me I have talent, everyone who's ever said I'm exceptional, everyone who's ever said they admired what I've accomplished—if they were all just, you know, being nice.

Which is ridiculous.

Of course, they were just being nice.

But I guess what I would tell you is that, wherever you are on your career timeline, wherever you are in your relationship with this thing you do for a living, you have to give yourself permission to grieve the end of something. And sometimes you have to work really, really hard to find what's next. I did *not* think it would be this hard. Maybe I was naïve. And maybe it's not this hard for everybody. Certainly I'm not the first one to jump without a net, and plenty of people move among jobs and careers, and they go from one thing to another, and they're good at all those things, and they relish them. Good on ya if you're that person! But don't worry about it if you're not.

And by the way, the next person who tells me "Just make it happen!" gets a punch in the face.

I do think it is wise, though, throughout your working life, to take time to reevaluate what you're doing, what you really love about it, and what you don't. I didn't do that very much. And I should have, *even* though I was in my dream job. Dream while you're in the dream.

So now I start over with that infernal question: What do I *want* to do? And how am I going to make that happen? And I'm not talking the mechanics—I know how to network and call the people who can help, and I know the resources that are available to me. Instead, it's about opening my heart and my head to what might be out there.

Maybe I can't live without microphones. I sure do love these things.

But I have already stepped off one cliff—the toughest one. So bring on the next one.

Bring on act 4.

What the hell are you doing?

I'm still figuring that out.

But one thing I *can* tell you is that it *will* be remarkable.

Thank you.

1.
SIGNING
OFF

Are you inspired now to take a flying leap from your career? Because, apparently, that's what happens after reading that speech.

Dozens of people have written to me in the last two years saying that because of the words I said on that stage in Portland, they *finally* decided to leave their jobs, even though they had no idea what would happen next. At first, as those letters flooded into my inbox, I thought, Uh oh, I don't want that responsibility. I don't want to be the reason you quit. Don't lay that on me!

But now? I'm excited for them. I cheer them on. I can't wait to see what they do next.

I wrote that speech in the middle of the night and in the wake of the greatest failure of my twenty-year career. I'd reached the point where I felt like I no longer had anything to lose, so why not just put it out there, my broken heart and soul on a platter, for nearly three thousand strangers. I told myself that after it was done, I'd just walk offstage and get back to figuring out what the hell I was going to do when I grew up. At that point, raw from rejection, I just didn't care anymore, for probably the first time, what people thought. I knew the audience probably wanted to hear positive messages—the ten steps to successfully quitting your job and how following your passion would lead to massive riches and happiness—but that's not what I gave them. What I delivered, instead, was the unvarnished suckage of my mental and emotional state at that moment. I gave them all my insecurity, doubt, and self-loathing over a span of thirty-five minutes that I figured would end in polite applause and then be instantly delivered into the annals of misanthropy.

That's not what happened.

Instead, it became one of those moments in life that you wish every soul on earth could experience. The acceptance of your story, your truth—the beautiful *and* the ugly—by people who want a little reality to cut through the rah-rah. The response was immediate and massive, and viral, far beyond any other piece of work I'd done in more than two decades in broadcasting and journalism.

And so now, here we are.

I wonder if *you* want to quit. If you do, I'm rooting for you. I can't say it has all worked out perfectly for me, but I've come to believe, without reservation, that no matter how hard it's been, it was the right thing to do. It took me about a year and a half after handing in my resignation letter to get to that point. But I believe that you know, deep in your belly, what you have to do and what's best for you. The hurdle you have to get over is the rest of your body, your head and your heart, which are actively telling you to ignore your gut. I interviewed about eighty people who had also left their careers without know-ing what they wanted to do next, and most of them had been ignoring their guts for months if not years. But we know when something is wrong.

There is some proof of this in a study known as the Iowa Gambling Task (IGT). In it, participants were given four decks of cards, all face down. Each card had a value—some with rewards and some with penalties. Some of the decks were stacked with low-value cards. The study measured intuition and how long it would take participants to realize that some of the decks were losers. It took most people forty to fifty flips before their brains relayed that something was amiss and they started choosing from the better decks of cards.

But the players were also hooked up to skin monitors that measured stress responses, such as sweat. And guess what? Their bodies started showing signs of stress after only ten flips, far in advance of when they fully processed the informa-tion. Your body knows something is up.

One of the most common questions I've been asked since I left my job is how to know when it's time to go. I can't an-swer that for you, and I don't think there's one answer for everyone—you are the only one who can figure out what's right for you. But if you're asking yourself the question, it's well past the time to start exploring the possibilities. And in all likelihood, your body is already showing you signs. For me, my hair stopped growing. For a good number of the people I interviewed, it was an unusual, and inexplicable, pain or other malady somewhere in their bodies. For some it was searing back pain, and for others it was exhaustion far beyond what could be explained by their work hours. I'm not a doctor, but I do know it's important to pay attention to those signals and to ask yourself whether they might be tied to your feelings about your work. Don't just ignore them.

So if you've had pangs about quitting, it's totally normal for it to take about forty rounds of cards with a stacked deck to get you to where I and all my fellow quitters were when we finally pulled the plug. But what you'll have that we didn't is a road map of the experience.

What's it like to leave a job you're still good at, still love, and can't imagine life without and to do it devoid of any idea of what you want to do next?

To start with, it's enough to make you sick.

III

The morning I had planned to hand in my resignation, I knew it was the mistake of a lifetime.

I knew it in the way you know there's something off about that piece of fish. I knew it in the way first-time bungee jumpers know for sure that this will be the one time the cord will slip loose from its knot on the way down. I knew it in the way you know that one more cocktail will make the next morning far brighter and louder than you'll want it to be.

I knew I shouldn't do this. I shouldn't quit. Every atom of my being was screaming at me. Flee your instincts! Run from this thing in your head and in your soul that is telling you to leave! You've got it way too good to walk away. You have your own national radio show. You have fans. You have a nice salary and a lifestyle to go with it. You love this work. This is your dream job. Don't do this. Don't. Do. This.

On the drive in to work that Wednesday, in August 2012, I felt sick. I'd been nauseous off and on for several days as I wrestled with the decision, and now I was sure that I was going to lose my breakfast (coffee and hard-boiled egg whites) on the twenty-minute commute from my home in Pasadena to the *Marketplace* studios in downtown Los Angeles. By the time I got to work, I not only felt sick to my stomach but I also felt dizzy. It was a Herculean task to keep from breaking down in tears.

Why would I break up the longest relationship I'd ever had? Especially when I had no backup plan in place.

I'd been in this relationship for nearly a quarter century, this love affair with radio journalism. And I was about to leap from that career.

I sat at my desk for an hour and a half before a scheduled meeting with my boss, the executive producer. I'd printed out my resignation letter at home and slipped it into a plain white envelope. I had plenty of things I should have accomplished in that hour and a half, but I did none of them. I kept imagining myself ripping up the letter in that fleeting way that your brain sometimes toys with driving off a bridge. But I left the envelope intact.

Just before the meeting, I sent an e-mail to my boss's bosses, telling them what I was about to do. It was a courtesy e-mail, since the week before, they had expressed dismay at rumors that I was thinking about leaving. I hit Send, got up from my chair, and walked the ten feet to my boss's office.

My entire body was shaking, as were the divorce papers in my hand.

Don't. Do. This.

III

People quit their jobs every day. They can't stand their managers, they're moving to another city, they want a shorter commute, they feel underpaid or unappreciated, they get a better offer, or sometimes they just want something else. In its most recent survey in 2012, the Bureau of Labor Statistics reported that the median employee tenure—the amount of time people spend in a given job—was about four and a half years. Surveys of the Millennial generation show its tenure expectation is less than three years.[i] Workers come and go all the time. There is nothing special about quitting.

My employee tenure record was 4-4-3-11—that is, the number of years I had spent in each job. I had quit three previous times in my post-college career. Each departure was difficult in its own way. Resigning isn't fun, because your departure leaves a hole in the organization. It makes life harder for your employers, and they don't generally relish that. And from your perspective as an employee, unless you absolutely hated the place, you probably have decent memories of the work you did there and the colleagues who surrounded you. It's neither fun nor easy. But it happens all the time.

Most people leave because they've found another opportunity. They're leaving one job and going to another. Sometimes that entails a move to a different city, as was the case for me twice. It always means change, because you're departing one set of coworkers and responsibilities for an entirely different set of personalities and work environments. All of that is enough to create anxiety and a sense of being unmoored, at least during the transition from one job to the next, and even through whatever ramp-up time is involved in getting acquainted with the new gig. But moving from one job to another is also a time of great anticipation and excitement, especially if it involves a promotion, a bump in compensation, and a change of scenery. What most people *don't* do is quit without knowing what's next. You're never supposed to do that without having a plan in place, right? It's not wise financially, it's a dumb move for your career, and it shows instability and a lack of commitment. At least that's what we're told from the moment we can grasp the concept of a career.

And yet, there I was. And although I've said there's nothing special about quitting, for me, this time—the fourth time— was different.

III

I first fell in love with public radio in 1987.

I was eighteen and a first-year journalism student at Northwestern University in Evanston, Illinois. I was 100 percent sure I wanted to go into television broadcasting. But a family friend offered to help me get a summer internship at Oregon Public Broadcasting (OPB) in my hometown of Portland. In the radio department. I had watched public television my entire life, from *Sesame Street, Mister Rogers' Neighborhood,* and *The Electric Company* as a kid, to the *MacNeil/Lehrer Newshour, 3-2-1 Contact,* and *Sneak Previews* as a teenager. I had never listened to public radio. I had no idea what *All Things Considered* was or *A Prairie Home Companion* or *Morning Edition*—but OPB offered the chance to work in a real newsroom, and that was enough.

I spent the first day learning what to watch for on the AP wire, which even in the late 1980s was still a teleprinter with bells that went off when there was urgent news. The producers also showed me how to use a Marantz tape deck (which was, back then, about the size of a small briefcase) and a microphone, and they gave me my first real reporter's notebook—the classic spiral-bound-at-the-top notebook, complete with the word *News* emblazoned across the front cover. Journalists of a certain age all remember the first time they held one. I felt official, even though I had no idea what I was doing.

The next day—the second day of my internship—during the morning meeting, the news director, Tom Goldman, glanced around the room at a summer-vacation-shrunken staff and looked over at me and said, "Tess, you go cover the library strike."

Multnomah County librarians were picketing downtown, and he wanted someone to get tape.

"Me?"

"Yeah, go. You have a car?"

"Yes."

He suggested I try to find a union rep and a librarian or two. He reminded me that once I had the interviews, I should check the tape to make sure it recorded. (This is a lesson many of us have had to learn the hard way after getting back to the studio and realizing that we had forgotten to hit Record or the microphone cord had shorted out.)

I didn't tell Tom that I'd gotten a C in my Basic Writing class at journalism school (a specialized class infamous for weeding out students who were never going to make it through the year in J school). I didn't mention that I had no idea how to walk up to strangers, stick a small pole in their face, and ask them questions they probably didn't want to answer.

Interns don't say no, so I went downtown, walked up to strangers, stuck a small pole in their face, and asked them questions about why they were on strike. Much to my surprise and delight, they answered those questions, and I had my first-ever radio tape.

When I got back to OPB, I assumed I would hand that tape off to another reporter to put together for broadcasting.

"OK, now write it up," Tom said after checking to see whether I, indeed, had audio on the tape recorder.

"Me?"

"Yeah, see what you can do with it."

It turned out that I had gotten a decent recording, so I transcribed pieces of it as I listened back, making note, as another producer had instructed, of where those pieces were on the tape recorder counter. With the help of newspaper and wire articles, I wrote up what was probably about a minute-long story with a tape cut or two, which was then edited down to about a thirty-second story with a shorter tape cut or two.

"OK, go into the studio and voice it," Tom said.

"Me?"

Yes. Me. And so, on my second day of my first internship, I was on the radio. By the end of the summer of 1987, after three months of on-air stories, I didn't want to be off the air.

III

But by college graduation day in June 1990, I had decided that I definitely, absolutely, wanted to go into *television* news. I had majored in broadcasting, which at Medill meant television (they didn't have a radio program you could major in, although I did work at the campus station), and I had enjoyed the field-work in those classes. The only downside of TV was that the equipment was heavy. And I was slightly put off when I pro-duced what I thought was a damn good story on the Illinois lottery, and my professor's primary comment was that I should have paid more attention to my blush; apparently, I was too pale in my on-screen reporter standups. But TV was where I wanted to be, and it was where everybody went when they desired fame and fortune, which I most certainly did.

After the graduation ceremonies, my mom accompanied me on the 2,100-drive to get my car from Chicago back home to Portland, and along the way we stopped at every small-market station where a news director had grumpily agreed to meet with me and watch my demo tape. We hit I-90 West with my Betamax tapes and one navy suit in the back of my black Ford Escort. This was how you were supposed to do the television news job search: call up producers, tell them you were in town, and ask if they would give you a critique, no promises of a job. Rockford, Illinois; Rochester, Minnesota; Sioux Falls, South Dakota; Casper, Wyoming; Idaho Falls, Idaho; and Pendleton, Oregon. Everyone I met was, for the most part, polite, though I inevitably heard the words "lose weight" more than I heard anything having to do with the content of my stories. I wasn't fat, but I was beyond the bounds of what you might call the classically attractive and fit broadcast news babe, even in the country's smallest media markets. (My weight had been an on-going struggle since the college freshman ~~fifteen~~ twenty.)

When we finally arrived home in Portland, no job in hand,

I decided to stop by the OPB studios, just to say hello to my old friends with whom I'd kept in touch since my internship. Would I ever come back to radio, some of them asked. Probably not, I said. I really got most of my training in television. Plus, I'd like to make some money, and that for sure will never happen in public radio, much as I love you guys.

I said that last part in my head.

Mom and I did another go-see trip through California. Same answer everywhere: we don't have any openings, thanks for stopping by, and maybe lose some weight. I arrived home dejected and unemployed and still living with my parents, which was unacceptable to me even though I was only a few weeks past graduation. I stopped in at OPB again to say hello, and my friends told me there was an opening for a reporter. Would I be interested?

In broadcast media, one way you know you're making progress in your career is by the size of the market you're in. Most broadcasters start out in, say, the 100th market, or smaller, usually the so-called one-man bands, where you are the reporter, editor, videographer, producer, and anchor, and probably the weather girl too. Once you've made your bones, you move up to a larger market, maybe 80th or 75th, and so on until you become the 6 p.m. anchor at the NBC affiliate in New York City, the number 1 market in the country. And then, of course, you get a spot on the *Today* show. So that's why I had been in all those small markets, begging them to let me sit there while they watched my demo tape and told me to lose weight. It's just what you did.

Portland, in 1990, was the 25th market. That's not where you would begin a broadcasting career, not even in radio. It is, or at least was, rare that anyone would get to skip ahead to the big markets after starting out in Portland for his or her first job.

I wanted to work. I wanted a paycheck, and I wanted to start savoring post-college independence. I'd had a plan—the one that was going to get me to the *Today* show, but it wasn't panning out at the speed I required of myself. So I handed my résumé to OPB radio's program director. A few days later they asked when I could start. It was late July, six weeks or so past graduation, and I had a job, in my chosen field of journalism, in the 25th media market, my hometown, with a salary of about $17,000.

Television could wait.

III

What I loved about public radio when I joined its ranks is what I love about it to this day: it's smart, it's evocative, and more than anything, it's intimate. Think about how you listen to the radio. You're probably by yourself, in a car, or with headphones on, and someone is telling you a story or sharing an idea or explaining something complex about the world. That person's voice is in your ear. It's *right there.* And if that person is good at it, it seems like he or she is talking to you, and only to you. I love that part of *listening* to radio, and it's my favorite part of *making* radio. When I'm in front of the microphone, either introducing a story or conducting an interview, I try to pretend there's only one person in the room with me, and we're just talking, just having a conversation. Everybody else is eavesdropping and using their imaginations to fill in the pictures.

Seven-second sound bites on television can't do that. Even the very best newspaper and magazine writing can't do that. The human voice establishes an intimate relationship almost immediately, and if you use it well, it will send an audience wherever you want them to go. In fact, in public radio, our holy grail is to prompt what we refer to as the "driveway moment," when you, as a listener, are so absorbed in what you're hearing that you sit in the car, with a trunk full of groceries (perhaps even melting ice cream), until that story is over.

When I fell in love with radio, I fell hard, and I fell fast. Shortly after I started at OPB, I sold my first network news spot to, incredibly, *Marketplace*. As a member-station reporter, I was allowed and encouraged to file as a freelancer for network programs, and my favorite public radio show asked for a three-minute feature story on the first Niketown. When the story aired, I remember listening in wonderment when my voice came on, introduced by then-anchor Jim Angle:

"From KOPB in Portland, Tess Vigeland has the story."

And at the end of the spot, these words from my own mouth:

"For *Marketplace*, I'm Tess Vigeland in Portland, Oregon."

Friends and family had to peel me off the ceiling. My first time on the national airwaves. And I was all of twenty-one years old.

It was beyond thrilling. I knew that's where I wanted to work. That's where I was meant to be. Now I had a plan, and I would make it happen. As for my dreams a few months earlier of making it happen in television. . . . Television? What's television?

| | |

I spent four years at OPB covering the environment, education, and the arts, among other subjects.

After the feature for *Marketplace*, a couple of months later, in early 1991, I filed my first newscast spot for NPR. I got a $25 check for a forty-five-second story about the large protests in downtown Portland against the Gulf War. I filed lots of stories for the network over the next few years, but my big break came in January 1994, with the assault of Olympic figure skater Nancy Kerrigan.

For those too young to remember, Kerrigan was one of the country's top figure skaters in the early 1990s. As she left the ice after a practice session at the U.S. Figure Skating Championships in Detroit in 1994, a man ran up to her and whacked her right knee with a police baton. Authorities soon unraveled a Keystone Cops–worthy conspiracy by the husband of one of Kerrigan's main on-ice rivals, Tonya Harding, to take Kerrigan out of the competition. The incident garnered intense national and international attention for months; as Kerrigan recovered, Harding found herself under FBI investigation, and she ended up pleading guilty to hindering the prosecution of her husband and two others who carried out the attack.

I was assigned to the story because Harding was from Portland. She trained at a suburban rink, and she was one of only a very few professional athletes to come out of the area, so she was well known locally. After Detroit, the national sports media hounded her and followed her around Portland, from her practice rink to her home to the FBI building downtown, and, later, to the federal courthouse. I was among that pack of media hounds, and NPR, for all its highfalutin, only-the-really-important-stories reputation, couldn't get enough. This was the story everyone wanted, and I filed story after story not just for NPR but also for the CBC in Canada and the BBC. I even did a phone interview with a station in Australia. It seemed as if I was filing a news spot every time Harding hiccupped.

At the same time as that scandal unfolded, Republican Bob Packwood, Oregon's junior senator, was accused of the serial groping of Capitol Hill staffers. I covered that story too, filing consistently for the network.

I found myself on national airwaves all the time. What was bad for Tonya Harding and Bob Packwood was a huge boon for my career visibility. I loved filing for NPR, and I loved the idea that people around the country heard my work. I loved the delight in my parents' voices when they told me of friends in far-flung states who had called up to say how great my stories were. I loved it every time my friends said over microbrew beers how cool it was to hear me on *All Things Considered*. I was in my element.

That summer, in 1994, OPB also tapped me to co-host a weekly public affairs program on the TV side of the station. I hadn't done television since college, but they asked me to audition with the male host they had in place, Jim Leinfelder. We were already good friends, and we had some on-air chemistry, so I thought it would be fun to see what public television is like. Jim and I debuted the weekly program, called *Seven Days*, to much fanfare and publicity by OPB. It was a heady time. I felt as if my star was rising.

Things weren't perfect though. I was four years into my career, and I was already feeling the itch to see what else might be out there in the vast world of public broadcasting. (Over the next twenty years, I'd realize that this particular world is not vast, but rather narrow and tiny. But I didn't know that then.) Despite the television opportunity, and because of various frustrations with management at OPB, I started applying for jobs in larger markets, bigger cities, hoping to make a jump that would get me on my way toward a gig with a national show—ideally, *Marketplace*. Out of the blue, I got a call from a station I never imagined would know I existed: WBUR in Boston. WBUR was one of the, if not *the*, flagship local stations in all of public radio. Its reporters were on network shows all the time. So, yeah, I wanted to work there. No question. Except that there was, actually, one question. A producer named David Greene wanted to know if I had any interest in reporting for a sports show. He might as well have lobbed a soccer ball at my forehead. I knew exactly nothing about sports, except basketball, because Dad had season tickets to the Portland Trailblazers, the only pro sports team in town. I was a proud arts department dork— theater, band, choir, and piano lessons from the age of five.

"Well, we're not really looking for people who know a lot about sports," David said over the phone.

Why not?

"This is a show about sports for people who think they don't care about sports, which is most of the public radio audience."

Why would you try to force a subject on people who don't like it? I heard myself talking myself out of a job.

"Well, we like sports, and we think listeners will tune in if we show them that sports is more than just box scores and locker room shoptalk. Pick almost any subject—money, politics, economics, art—and you can see it in sports. That's what we're covering. And NPR wants to pick up the show. And Bill Littlefield is our host."

Now, I'd heard Bill's sports commentaries on NPR for years, and I always stopped whatever I was doing to listen to them. Because they weren't really about sports. They were about life. They were about life's issues and problems, victories and defeats, ugliness and beauty. His writing was beyond sublime, and he had a voice hand-crafted by the gods of radio.

So, yes, now I *really* wanted to work there. I got the job, moved to Boston, and joined what some journalists dismissively call the Toy Department. But now that I've covered sports, I'm pretty sure other parts of the newsroom call it that because they're envious. Who doesn't want to play with toys for a living? I spent hours on end watching ESPN and learning all I could about this new subject. My inaugural assignment for *Only A Game* (OAG), which by then was a nationally syndicated show heard on more than a hundred stations, was a brief interview with The Greatest. Muhammad Ali was ten years into his battle with Parkinson's disease, and he had trouble speaking, but I knelt next to his chair, asked a couple of questions about an award he was receiving, and he said a few words into my microphone. It was another one of those moments I've had so often in my career where I think to myself, "Am I really doing this? Am I really sitting next to and talking with Muhammad Ali? Why, yes. Yes, I am. And most people in this world can't say they've ever done that." Sure, I was a little nervous, but mostly, I was giddy, and I enjoyed every one of those few moments, realizing that as a national sports reporter, I would probably have more of them, and my delight in that was a clear sign that I belonged here. Not a bad first day at the office.

For the next two years I had a front-row seat to some of the highs and lows of sports history. I covered the Major League Baseball strike of 1994–95, including spring training in Florida where long-haul truckers were among those who tried out to be replacement players. I was there when Magic Johnson un-retired from the NBA and then retired again. One day there was a football team in Cleveland; the next day it moved to Baltimore. Cincinnati Reds owner Marge Schott was run out of baseball for racially "insensitive" remarks (nearly twenty years before LA Clippers owner Donald Sterling was run out of basketball for the same reason). I attended the very first ESPN X Games in Rhode Island, where I struggled to explain the concept of "street luge," and I braved the snows of Lake Placid for a marvelously loony profile of British ski jumper Eddie "The Eagle" Edwards while he trained for an Olympic comeback. Tiger Woods revived the game of golf on my watch. And I was at Camden Yards when fans gave Baltimore Orioles short-stop Cal Ripken a twenty-two-minute standing ovation as he played in his 2,131st consecutive game, surpassing a record set decades earlier by Lou Gehrig and setting a new standard for tenacity and dedication in sports. (My story started with this sentence: "There were tears, even in the press box.") I came to appreciate, and even love, this subject I'd really known nothing about until my mid-twenties.

The show's host, Bill Littlefield, was easily the biggest influence of my career when it came to writing for radio. Each and every week, Bill just told stories. He wrote exclusively, and exquisitely, for the ear, and he was never shy about letting listeners hear his delight in what he was doing. That's what I learned most from Bill and what I tried to emulate throughout my career: let them hear your delight. In other words, be real.

His love of what he was doing, both on and off the air, made *me* want to host a show.

And, in fact, that's exactly what I did when Bill was out. We hadn't officially established that I would be his backup when the show brought me to Boston, but within a few months, the producers asked me to guest host, and I became the regular backup whenever Bill was out. I don't know who filled that role before I joined the show, probably a reporter from the newsroom, but for the rest of my time there, I was it. So I got a taste of what it was like to be in The Big Chair, to be the main voice, the driver, of a program. There was more freedom in hosting than in reporting, where you have to be so much more detached, and I was hooked pretty quickly on the spotlight that came with that job.

In my time working for OAG, my long-term plan evolved. While I loved being with OAG and I enjoyed learning about and covering sports, I was still a loyal listener to *Marketplace*, and I still dreamed of one day working for that show. There were similarities between the two—they both deal in specialized subjects (sports, economics) that the general population doesn't necessarily think they'll find interesting, and both shows had a real personality that stood out from the regular news programs that you heard elsewhere on public radio. In a word, they both sounded *fun*. But I didn't think sports would hold my attention for any more than two to three years, and I longed for the day that not only would I work at *Marketplace* but I would also be a host at *Marketplace*. Rarified air, that is. But it was now on the list. It was part of The Plan.

After two years at OAG, I moved over to the WBUR newsroom to become a general assignment reporter. I covered an entire waterfront of topics, from the New England mob trials to a trip through the bowels of Boston's Big Dig, from the April Fool's Blizzard of 1997 (three feet of snow in twenty-four hours) to the annual sailing of the USS *Constitution—Old Ironsides—* across Boston Harbor. One of the greatest joys of journalism is meeting people most other people don't get to meet, going places most other people don't get to go, and doing things most other people don't get to do. You don't have to get a license to be a reporter (though sometimes I wonder if we'd all be better off), but being a reporter is a license to follow through on pretty much whatever makes you curious. And that means every day is different. You cannot be bored as a general assignment reporter. I continued to fill in as the host when the calls came, this time during the local broadcasts of *Morning Edition* and *All Things Considered*. And while I liked being a reporter, more and more, I got hooked on anchoring.

III

I've always said that there are three elements that make up the perfect job: you work with and for people who respect you, you're compensated appropriately, and you love your work. At OPB and WBUR I had various combinations of the first and last of those. But after four years at WBUR, I was starting to feel the itch again. The joys of the job had started to fade a bit, in part because of the culture in the newsroom and in part because I wasn't hosting enough and I missed that chair. I was also, I think, at a point in my career where I, unexpectedly, wondered what other opportunities might be available to me—in particular, more lucrative opportunities. You don't go into public radio to make money. Public stations are nonprofits, and as a general rule, the salaries reflect that reality. I was in my late twenties and I had a cool job, but the job barely paid the rent in a city as expensive as Boston. I wondered if I could be happy doing something I liked less as long as it paid more. So I left journalism for a public relations job in the private sector, almost doubled my salary, and stayed there for three years, enjoying the money and my colleagues, but not the work.

I continued freelancing, if for no other reason than because I didn't want to lose my radio chops and I didn't want people to forget me. My husband, whom I'd met when he was an audio engineer and I was a reporter at WBUR, was transferred to Ireland for six months in his new capacity as a software consultant, and I went with him, covering the Northern Ireland peace talks at Stormont in the fall of 1999, as well as stories in and around the Emerald Isle.

Still, the shock was genuine the day I got a call—in late spring 2001—from a producer at . . . *Marketplace!*

"We have a job opening that we're wondering if you'd be interested in. Host of the *Marketplace Morning Report*. Are you familiar with the show?"

I hated to say it, but . . . no. I knew *Marketplace* but not the *Morning Report*.

"It's a series of short business newscasts that's offered to stations in the E segment of *Morning Edition*. The casts are about eight minutes long, featuring whatever's happened overnight while people were sleeping."

The E segment of *Morning Edition* is the part that runs from ten-of-the-hour to the top of the hour. I didn't know about the *Marketplace Morning Report* (MMR) because WBUR covered up the E with its own material from staff reporters and it didn't carry the *Marketplace* feed. I thanked her for getting in touch with me, and then I asked whether it would entail a move to *Marketplace* headquarters in Los Angeles.

"Yes, you'd need to move. All of our programs are produced in LA. And you should know that because of the time difference between the West Coast and Wall Street, MMR is an overnight shift. You're on the air when the East Coast wakes up."

Los Angeles? Graveyard shift? Did I really want to get up in the mid—

Oh, shut up. Of course you do. It's *Marketplace!*

I was gobsmacked. I couldn't believe this was happening. *Marketplace* was calling *me*, and I wasn't even technically in radio anymore.

My husband knew my goals and ambitions, and he didn't even blink when I said I was interested in possibly moving to LA to work at *Marketplace.* We worried a bit about what it meant for his software consulting job, which required quite a bit of travel throughout the northeastern United States. But he said that we'd figure it out and that he knew it was important for me to pursue my dream. That generosity of spirit, and recognition of the importance I attached to my career, endures to this day.

So I went to LA and auditioned. A couple of weeks later, the program's then-executive producer, J. J. Yore, called and offered me the job as a host at *Marketplace.* I had vowed, I had made plans, and I had set goals to someday achieve that status in my career. I had worked hard for years to prove myself as a reporter and anchor. And then I left the industry and assumed the dream was no longer even a remote possibility. Instead, my dream job *called me.* Eleven years into my career, I was going to be an anchor at the national radio show I had idolized from the very beginning. And I was only thirty-two years old. I was meant to do this. I was meant to work at *Marketplace.* It didn't even matter that I had gone off course. The career I was always supposed to have had come back to me. If that was not a sign from the universe that I was on the right track, I'm not sure what would be.

So, yes, quitting happens all the time. It's not special.

But for me, eleven years after that call from *Marketplace,* it was.

III

As I walked into my boss's office that August morning in 2012, I asked myself, again, what the hell I was doing. "I love public radio. I really, truly love it," I thought. "I'm supposed to be here. I've been doing this for more than two decades. I'm one of those lucky people who's always known what she was put on this earth to do. No searching for the right career. I've had exactly the right career. And I got to the place I wanted to go. I'm here. I'm at *Marketplace.*"

Still, with every fiber of my being screaming at me not to do it, I handed over the white envelope containing my workplace divorce papers.

I could feel my throat tightening up the way it does before you start choking on your sobs. But I held it together and just waited.

My boss didn't say much and barely skimmed the letter.

"Are you sure about this?"

Yes.

"You know this is not what I wanted to happen."

I stood silently.

"Can you give us a couple of days to put together a press release and staff announcement before you tell anybody?"

Sure.

"OK. If we could get a quote from you for the release . . ."

I gave a quote, and I also gave them three months before I would leave so that they could train a replacement host. And that was pretty much it. I had built up all kinds of drama in my head. But it was just quiet. And deeply, profoundly sad.

III

Three months later, on my last day, the Friday before Thanksgiving, I normally would have taped my final show during our usual 9 a.m. show roll. But that show, my last, was part of the program's partnership with the *New York Times*, and we had preproduced it earlier in the week to accommodate the paper's publication deadline. Mine was the cover story for the special section, featuring a series of stories from survivors of a terrible tornado in Missouri, telling what they had learned about financial emergency preparedness.[2]

So I had nothing to do that day but pack up my office. I took down the large frame full of press passes from my time as a sports reporter. I took down the framed copy of my first *New York Times* byline. I had stacks and stacks of books from eleven years of author interviews, and I transferred those to a shelf in another part of the newsroom. I had all manner of holiday-themed candy dishes to pack up, because for most of the time I was at *Marketplace*, I would decorate my office for holidays and put out, say, green and red M&M's for staff snack attacks. The large orange plastic jack-o'-lantern was consistently raided and filled and raided again during the last two weeks of October.

I had more public radio mugs than any one person should be allowed to stash on a desk (Call now with your pledge!) and all manner of tchotchkes given to me by people I'd interviewed over the years: a lucky toy turtle from the ladies of a Virginia investment club I'd spent a year profiling, a glass-encased candle from the author of a book about the aftermath of Hurricane Katrina, handwritten letters from listeners who took the time to say how much they appreciated our show. I kept all of those.

Just before leaving, I went around the office and said my good-byes, willing myself not to get emotional.

But after I put the last box in the trunk of my car and walked back into the office for what was, in fact, the last time, I teared up. I looked around, took a photo of the iconic MARKET-PLACE sign in the reception area, and sobbed one more time on the way out of the building.

III

At this point you may have surmised that the circumstances behind my departure weren't of the positive kind—instead, they were a malignant combination of thwarted innovation, bruised ego, ambition fatigue, and plain-old boredom. Yes, I joked in the World Domination Summit speech that I would tell the full story when I published my memoirs, but, really, it's not important anymore. I played just as much a role in my unhappiness as anyone else had, and it had become time for me to go. There's nothing to gain from spilling dirt, but there's everything to lose in doing so.

Maybe I was brave, but in many ways I was also stupid. Quitting has worked out so far, but there's a lot more to consider than I did before leaping. I'll take you through several of those considerations so that you don't go blindly into that void. I've tried and tried, but I can't really describe what happened in my head the day I made the decision to quit, and what allowed me to do so, especially when I'm far from being the world's most confident person. But again, I think you just know when it's time to go, and you simply must listen to that instinct.

Of course I'd also told myself I would have three months before I would have to get another job. Wouldn't you know it, though, those three months between the day I quit and my last day on the job were pretty much the busiest of my entire career. I threw myself into several big projects, including election-related road shows for *Marketplace* at several public stations across the country and a long piece for the *New York Times* that also required travel. I think I actively ignored the fact that I was about to be unemployed, and it was easier to do that if I kept myself as busy as possible. I also didn't want to change my mind. And more than anything, I wanted to leave on a high note. The highest note possible. I worked my butt off and turned out some of our best shows of the year—in my humble but considered opinion. On my way out the door, I wanted to show just how valuable I was and, I hoped, just how much I would be missed. Of course, in the end, we all find out that we are replaceable.

So, no, I did *not* line up my next job before leaving *Marketplace*. I didn't even look for one. And guess what? I still haven't gotten a full-time job. And for all kinds of reasons, that's OK.

Let's talk about what it's like to be OK with not having a job, or at least a plan, for me and some other good people who've taken giant leaps . . . without a net.

2.
OH
SH!T

My last day at *Marketplace* was a Friday, and for a whole weekend I felt euphoric. I partied with friends. I reveled in the idea that I wouldn't have to get up at 6 a.m. on Monday. Or Tuesday. Or any day for that matter, at least until I got a new job. I felt proud that I'd walked away from something I loved but that wasn't working anymore. I marveled that I had taken myself off track, after living a work life that was one steady, planned ride. This was so out of character for me, and I loved that I seemed to be breaking my own mold. I had no plan, and it was *great*!

Until Monday. When I realized that I had no plan. And that's when quitting became *not* great.

That post-leap moment when you *really* absorb the idea that you have no idea what to do next? That's not a fun moment. It smells like failure. And idiocy.

Wendy Harris stepped off the track after a successful career as a securities litigator. She left her job because she felt a pull to do something more meaningful, though she wasn't sure what that would be. Also, she said, she was looking for a more supportive working environment. "Law firms are not warm-and-fuzzy places generally." She had taken an earlier sabbatical, but it wasn't enough, and she realized, after returning to her firm, that she craved a more permanent change.

When I asked her what the first few days were like after quitting, her words were an echo of my own. "I was so euphoric," she said, "that I couldn't stop smiling! I would just take off that first week, I had said. I would take it as a vacation, and I would not do anything. And then I woke up Monday morning, and I was like, good Lord, what have I done? After that, I had these days when in the same day I would think, This is great. This is totally going to work out. I can do this! And then literally five hours later, I was asking, What am I doing? I don't know what I'm doing, and I don't know who I am anymore."

It is culturally ingrained in us to be uncomfortable with the idea of not having a plan. It's a foreign concept. Most of us go through life with one or more plans, and we base our notions of success in large part on whether we've followed those plans and met those goals. Suddenly being without one is uncomfortable in the extreme, especially when all of the advice around this topic says that you *must* figure out everything before you make a change.

Carl Seidman had the same tug-of-war with himself, only he put it off for a while after his last day at work. He's a corporate turnaround and restructuring consultant in Chicago who also handles crisis management, and he had spent several years with a Big Four accounting firm. He had left his job a little less than a year before we met. "The first three months were absolutely mesmerizing," he said. "I was in South America by myself for most of it and just feeling on top of the world. I just had this peace of mind, and I was seeing how other people in other countries and other cultures live, which is so, so important. When I got back, I looked around and wondered, 'Why is everybody looking at their smartphones? Just smile and sit down and eat a taco!' But I was also asking myself, 'Holy sh*t, what do I do now? I'm going to be sitting at home all day. I have to make my own schedule because nobody is going to tell me I have to be at work at eight o'clock or nine o'clock—it is really hard to create my own life!' It's just so ridiculous that here is this thing I had aspired to have, to be my own boss, to be in charge of my own destiny, and I had no clue what to do. But wait, do I have to know what I'm doing? Why do I need a path? Why do I need a plan? No, I need to get on the path. No, you shouldn't be doing that; you should do this instead!"

The good news is that Wendy, Carl, and I, and most of the other people I've spoken with, were not irretrievably off track, even though we all felt like we were. Career transition is a topic of study for Herminia Ibarra, a professor at the INSEAD business school in France. She's the author of a book called *Working Identity: Unconventional Strategies for Reinventing Your Career*, as well as several papers about people leaping from jobs. When I talked with her, I shared how difficult it had been to deal with the reality that hit a few days after my departure, and I asked why people feel so compelled to have a plan in place before leaving a job. "Because they've been told that's the thing to do," she said. "Because they're scared of what's going to happen and [they don't know] who's going to pay the bills, everything that you'd expect. The job market is not exactly easy these days. After that, the psychological factors come in. They don't know where they belong, they don't know how to describe what they do and who they are, and it's very scary."

This is a key factor, this notion of identity, and it's directly tied to our obsession with having a plan. We stick to a plan so we can stick to being the person we've become. I didn't pick up on that for several months. I couldn't figure out why I felt so unmoored. I could still work, I wasn't a different person, and as far as I was concerned, all I had lost was a salaried day job (which is still a big deal, but it's just a job). But in truth, I had lost so much more. As I said in my WDS speech, I was no longer "*Marketplace*'s Tess Vigeland." I was just Tess Vigeland. Wendy and Carl had lost so much more too. We had all lost a core identity. In her book, Ibarra says that in changing careers, you are essentially changing your identity. And *that* is a much longer, messier, and more intense process than anyone realizes, and it can cause enormous amounts of stress if you don't see it coming.

I didn't see it coming. I did not realize how much of my sense of self was wrapped up in my plan, in executing that plan, and in becoming the Tess Vigeland I had always known I was meant to be, forever and a day, when I finally made it to *Marketplace*.

III

Once I had gotten the anchor job at the *Marketplace Morning Report,* it wasn't long before I started looking down the road at what the next two-, five-, and ten-year plans entailed. Someday, *someday,* I would be the host of *Marketplace*, which is public radio's flagship daily business and economics program. I knew it would take a *very* long time to achieve that goal, and I figured once I achieved it, it would be the place I would stay, the show I would host, the rest of my working life, because for me, it didn't get any bigger than hosting *Marketplace*. This would be my World Series, my Van Cliburn, my Oval Office.

After I got the *Morning Report* job, my husband, Dan, and I made a recon trip to LA in August 2001 to find an apartment. It was also my chance to sell him on the idea of being in Los Angeles. How did I do that? I rented a red convertible Ford Mustang, of course, so we could drive with the top down around Santa Monica and Venice while we found a place to live in our new city. He decided this might not be so bad after all. Maybe LA wasn't just gangs and freeways.

We found a place in Marina del Rey, about two blocks from the ocean, and then headed home to pack up our apartment in Boston. Our plan was to send a truck with our stuff to the West Coast and to follow a week or so later by plane. So we booked a flight for the second week in September.

American Airlines. Flight 11. Boston to Los Angeles.

September 14, 2001.

III

The day the terrorists' planes hit the World Trade Center and the Pentagon was supposed to be my last day at my PR agency job in Boston. When I got to the office, just before 9 a.m., several people were crowded around a bank of TVs in the reception area. At first they said a small aircraft had hit the Empire State Building, but it quickly became clear that this was far more serious. TV commentators were still trying to piece it together. And then the second tower was struck.

We watched that one live. People started crying. Nobody could understand how these accidents could happen at the same time. And then the word *terrorism* started to surface.

Nobody knew what to do or say. This was Boston, so lots of people had friends and relatives in New York, not to mention that the planes had left from Logan International Airport and there was a chance that some of them knew people who were flying that day. You could feel the tension rising in the office. My boss, Norman Birnbach, and I went to his office and turned on the TV. When NBC Pentagon correspondent Jim Miklaszewski came on the air to say he'd just heard some sort of explosion, that's when I started crying. I looked at Norman, with both hands covering my mouth, left his office, and called my mother on the West Coast, who hadn't heard any of the news yet.

Within an hour of the planes' hitting in New York City, the mayor of Boston announced a mandatory, precautionary evacuation of all high-rises in the city. That included our building, so we all left. I didn't know where to go or what to do. Dan and I were bunking with his brother and sister-in-law while the moving truck made its way to LA, so "home" was an hour's train ride south of the city. We had sold our car already, figuring we'd buy a new one once we got to LA. Like everyone else in the world, I was utterly distraught and wanted to *do* something, so I called up Sam Fleming, the news director at my former employer WBUR, and said, "If you need help, I'm available." He told me, yes, come to the station, and we'll put you to work. They needed all the help they could get at that point.

When I got there, they gave me recording equipment and said to go to the corporate headquarters for TJX, the parent company of T.J.Maxx stores, located in Framingham, Massachusetts. Seven of its employees were on American Airlines Flight 11, bound for LA, which had crashed into the North Tower of the World Trade Center. I drove to Framingham and joined the scrum of reporters waiting outside the company's front doors for comment. Unsurprisingly, and completely justifiably, none came. So the assignment desk sent me a few miles away to the Massachusetts Emergency Management Agency bunker where state police had stashed the acting governor, Jane Swift. I covered the short news conferences officials gave from there, then returned to the station and worked late into the night to prepare stories for the next morning. It wasn't much, but it let me feel as if I was at least a very small part of what was easily the biggest, worst, and saddest story of a lifetime.

Journalists have a need to be a part of things. It's what I missed most when I left WBUR for the private sector, that sense of involvement. I'm not sure that need, that lust for the story, ever goes away. It becomes a part of you, part thrill, part curiosity, part busybody nosiness, and part desire to help explain and provide context for what's happening in the world. That's the draw of being a reporter. You want to be there for all the big stories, even the ones that make you sob in agony. I was relieved to pick up a microphone and do the job on the day that no one will ever forget.

III

While the world was reeling from the events of that Tuesday morning, Dan and I had the trivial-in-context, yet very real to us, issue of figuring out how we were going to get to LA. Airports nationwide were shut down for who knew how long. We had sold our car. Trains were booked, and rental cars were all gone by the time we got around to realizing our situation. So on Thursday, September 13, we bought a car. It was an odd thing to do in the middle of a cataclysm, and there were no other customers in the entire showroom, but we couldn't think of another solution. We picked it up early the next morning, packed in all our belongings that hadn't made it onto the moving truck, plus two cats in the back, and drove it off the lot and onto the freeway and across the country. We covered three thousand miles in four days, stopping only for gas, food, and lodging.

III

My first day of work at *Marketplace* was September 24, almost two weeks after 9/11. The stock market had reopened by then, but there was nothing normal about anything. It was a bizarre time to join a news staff, to jump into reporting on the economy, and to figure out how I was supposed to be feeling about ... everything. I had accomplished my primary career goal in what I considered record time, I was at this place I'd dreamed of for more than a decade, I'd be broadcasting daily to a national audience, I was living in an exciting new city, and honestly I could not have been more fortunate, proud, and beside myself with joy. Except I couldn't really feel any of those things, because they weren't important. They didn't matter. I didn't matter. The last thing you can afford to do is think about yourself at times like that, so the dream that I was in the middle of fulfilling took a backseat to the practicalities of figuring out where I fit in, what I was supposed to do, and how I was supposed to do it.

I also arrived to a changed, and chastened, *Marketplace*. The show I knew, the show I wanted to be a part of, the fun, light, airy program that somehow found a way to make money and economics interesting, was gone. This show was entirely serious and down to business. It was trying to figure out what its identity was, now that it couldn't be its former jaunty self. The rest of the world was trying to figure out if anything would ever be the same again, if this was the new normal forever, and *Marketplace* wasn't immune from that self-scrutiny. Social commentators had proclaimed the death of irony, satire, and whimsy. *Marketplace* trafficked in brilliant iterations of all three. It was a strange time to start a new job. But as a journalist, it was also the best time, because if there was one thing every single person needed, it was information. All the information they could possibly absorb—that's what the public longed for. And every journalist works to feed that longing, so there was no better time for me to return to the news.

The staid aura remained for a few weeks, but, slowly, *Marketplace* brought back its sense of self. Jocularity? No. Wit in the service of knowledge? Yes.

And there was a lot of information to share. The financial chicanery of the giant energy company Enron became public knowledge about five weeks after 9/11. Our newsroom quickly had to learn the ins and outs of energy swaps and mark-to-market accounting, and we watched as Enron's stock price plummeted to less than a dollar per share by the end of November. Following closely on Enron's heels were other massive accounting frauds at giant companies like WorldCom, Adelphia, Global Crossing, and Tyco among others (oh—and let's not forget Martha Stewart's being busted for insider trading). It seemed as if a CEO was getting hauled off in handcuffs for a perp walk before the cameras at least once a week! In the old *Marketplace* spirit, I launched a regular feature on *Marketplace Morning Report* (MMR) that I called the "Marketplace Crime Blotter," complete with the theme from *Dragnet*.

This was why I wanted to work here. Now we were having some fun. Not that we weren't a serious news operation, but there was finally some room for expressing the absurdity of what was happening in corporate America, and we had the freedom to do so. And I was finally reveling in the fact that I was there, on air, anchoring a national show, and loving every minute of it. Except the hours—I was not loving the alarm that woke me up at 3:30 each morning. But for the first couple of years, it was tolerable because I was doing what I always wanted to do.

Eventually, the real magic happened. I was tapped to fill-in host the Big Show—*Marketplace*, the half-hour afternoon show that was, still is, and always will be, the mothership. I can't remember why the regular backup hosts weren't available, but I finally made it to my ultimate goal. The Big Chair.

Marketplace goes up live at 2 p.m. Pacific time every weekday, in time for afternoon rush hour on the East Coast. That feed goes out to hundreds of thousands of listeners across the country, and you don't get a do-over during the show roll. Afterward there might be fixes for stations that air the program later, but in that half hour at 2 p.m., you're live.

Now, live radio didn't faze me. I'd been doing it for years at OPB and WBUR, and for MMR. I'm a professional, and I know when the "On-Air" light goes on, it's real, and everyone can hear me. *Marketplace* has theme music that rolls for a few seconds, then there's a funding credit, the host does a short introductory segment called a "billboard," and then the music comes back for a little bit before the show's introduction and first story. I wasn't nervous, per se, that first time, but I was a bit stunned that I was sitting in that seat. And in between the billboard and the start of the show, I started to choke up. I was so overwhelmed by where I was and what I was doing, and almost disbelieving that it was happening, that in those very few seconds, I almost couldn't get the words out. As a professional, it was nightmarish; as a person, it was human. I gathered myself in time, and no one had any idea how emotional I had just become for a scant few seconds, but it was as close as I've ever come to not being able to get words out over the air, even with a script right in front of me.

At that moment, I had it all. Everything I had worked for and wanted. I'd been there about three years at that point, and there I was, fulfilling the goal I had set so many years earlier. Sure, it wasn't my chair permanently, but it was a major step in the right direction. On the downside, though, it made me antsy for more. I started asking about getting off the morning shift. It was a risky and tough thing to do, because if I left MMR, it meant leaving the host chair. There weren't more host positions available, unless I wanted to go somewhere else within the parent company, which I didn't. There was no way I was leaving *Marketplace*.

But I was also exhausted. The graveyard shift is brutal, and I never handled it well physically, even though I loved the job itself. So after multiple discussions with my bosses—and they were not pleased that I was jumping ship from the overnight shift, because that's not an easy slot to fill—they agreed to let me return to reporting. Of course, I didn't love that nearly as much as the anchor seat, but I wanted off overnights, and at that point, it was my only option, so I took it. I also spent about six months in management, filling in for a senior producer who was on maternity leave.

About a year after leaving *Morning Report*, another host position opened up at *Marketplace*, on the weekend program that was dedicated to the personal side of finance, instead of the broader subjects of business and economics. I expressed immediate interest in the gig, despite its relatively small audience and stature as a weekend show, and despite the fact that I really had no interest in personal finance. As in *none*. But I was desperate to get the host chair again. Fortunately, I was named host of *Sound Money*, later renamed *Marketplace Money*, in January 2006.

I was back on the air. With my own national radio show. And for the next six years, that was just as it was meant to be.

The plan worked.

III

The biggest problem with ambition is that nothing you achieve ever feels like enough. We applaud ambition more than almost any other characteristic in the workplace. But sometimes, ambition butts up against a ceiling (oftentimes made of glass) that makes it very difficult to see how you can keep pushing for more.

Anyone looking from the outside would say I had a most

remarkable career. And in going back through it for this book, I'd have to agree! But it never felt like it while I was in it. The entire time I was at OPB, I wanted to be in a bigger market. The entire time I was at WBUR, I wanted to be with a national show. The entire time I was at *Marketplace*, even when I was hosting two separate national shows, I wanted to anchor the *Marketplace* afternoon program. I was never satisfied with being where I was, and as a general rule, that is a personality trait that's valued by most businesses. They want you hungry, they want you to be striving for bigger things, they want you to always be pushing yourself toward the next goal, the next career marker.

But I wasn't very good at simply enjoying what I achieved, because I was too busy keeping my eye on the next rung of the ladder.

When I became the host of *Marketplace Money* (MM) in 2006, you would think I'd have felt like I had really made it—accomplished that goal I had set out for myself more than a decade earlier.

In the back of my mind, though, as it always was, was the idea that this would be a holding pen for me until the host of *Marketplace*, then (and now) Kai Ryssdal, left someday. Whether that would be in five years or ten or twenty, I didn't care. I had wanted that spot from the moment David Brancaccio stepped down and David Brown was handed the job. I had wanted that spot from the moment David Brown stepped down and Kai was handed the job. I had tenure. I had an audience. I never had any indication that my on-air performance was less than exceptional. So at every opportunity, including annual goal setting, I said, "I want to be the first female host of *Marketplace*." Full stop. Each time, my boss smiled and said he appreciated my ambition and that we'd see what the future might bring. But there was no indication that he, or anyone else in the company, really thought of me as an heir apparent or successor of any sort.

The easy way for me to deal with this would have been to simply be grateful for the awesome job that I did have and make it entirely my own and embrace everything about it. I knew that I was lucky—scratch that, fortunate—scratch that, I had earned it. But it did feel like a consolation prize. And just because you get the consolation prize doesn't mean you stop trying for the brass ring.

I had my dream job, but I also didn't. I've described it like that—and it was pretty damn close. But I wanted more, and I swore that I would stick around long enough for that to happen, even though I probably should have taken the hint from all the times I had heard "We'll see." Nobody who management considers to be on the fast track gets a "We'll see" as often as I did.

III

So the writing was probably on the wall. That brass ring would not be mine. If I wanted to keep climbing, I'd need to do it somewhere else. But year after year, I stayed, even during times of great frustration and stasis, because who would be stupid enough to leave that job? Close-but-no-cigar is better than the alternative, which is to be nowhere near the cigar box. So I stayed. I wasn't miserable, but I wasn't particularly happy or satisfied or challenged. (I tried not to let this show at work— sometimes I succeeded, sometimes I didn't—and I never, *ever* let it show on air.) I certainly didn't want to go through the process of looking for another job, because I just knew there was no way I'd find something even close to a job as good as this one. Plus I was lazy.

This, according to author and career researcher Herminia Ibarra, is classic pre-leap behavior. "This is a messy process," she told me. "People don't know how to do it, and they don't want to fumble through it, and they don't know what they want to do, so they just stay where they are until one of two things happens: one, they get fired, something breaks the camel's back, or two, it just gets to the point where they're so miserable that they start moving their butt and doing anything they can. Because we don't move if we don't have to unless there's real pain there." And pain, she says, can cause paralysis, so waiting for it doesn't really do much good.

And how do you define "pain" anyway? It's impossible because it's different for me than it would be for you. And for me, it was drawn out, and I either didn't want to recognize it or I refused to acknowledge it. I pushed through because (a) the news never stops, and (b) I felt like what I was doing was important and helpful for people, and I couldn't just give up on it—or them. The financial crisis of 2008, its causes, and its aftereffects, consumed most of my time at the helm of MM. Unemployment woes, stock market worries, and the foreclosure mess endured for years. The whole event shook people to their core about the role of money management in their lives and the importance of planning for catastrophes not necessarily of their own making. There were lessons we'd tried to teach before things fell apart, and we kept trying to teach them after the worst had passed.

But it was always the same lessons, week in and week out. It was the same show for most of the six years I hosted. We tried to find ways to overhaul the format—I never liked having a call-in in the middle of a news magazine show—but when we tried real change, the powers-that-be always decided that it was too risky to lose the audience that loved whatever part of the program we were trying to change. That was especially true in my final few months, when I had a new senior producer who, like me, wanted to try some inventive, unusual, and fun programming that would have taken MM in a new direction. It became clear that was never actually going to happen.

These were the seeds of dissatisfaction that had been festering, probably from the moment I said yes to a job that I saw as merely a temporary answer to my ambitions. Unhappiness feeds on itself, and it creates stress you sometimes aren't even aware you have. By the summer of 2012, I knew something had to change, but I also knew I didn't want to leave. This was my dream job, or as close to it as I was probably going to get for a while. But at the same time, as I said in my speech, you eventually realize that it's time to leave, when you have too much self-respect to stay.

"But what about your plan?" you're asking. "Don't you have to have one?"

That's what we're told. That's what I preached on my own show. If you're going to leave a job, make sure you have another one lined up. Figure out what comes next before leaving your past behind.

But that's not what I did. And I'm far from the only one who did it differently and against all common sense advice.

Ibarra told me there are two ways that people go about a career transition:

1. *Plan and implement.* This is the traditional way we're told to make a change. "Let me figure out what I was meant to do, what's my purpose in life, my passion, get the answer clear, and then just go and do it. Find the network threads, and select the course and whatever it takes to implement it." But this, she says, presumes that you can figure out ahead of time that you know what that purpose in life is, which is *not* the case for most people whom she studied. "They couldn't get started because they didn't know."

2. *Experiment and learn.* This can happen while you're in a current job or, as was true for me and others I've talked to, after you leave one. "Go out and do stuff. Get involved in projects. Start, any way you can, in your community. Develop a nose for what interests you, read more broadly, talk to people you find interesting. A lot of times people think there's just going to be an opportunity that comes their way, that some serendipitous thing will happen. But that happens only if you're really broadening your network and doing things outside the day job. Otherwise it just won't occur."

This second approach is what Ibarra calls "working identity"—and here *working* is a verb, not an adjective. You are *working* your identity, working *into* a new one, instead of deciding what you're going to do first. "Doing comes first, knowing second," she writes in one of her papers. I put it this way: leap before you look. That turns a lot of career advice on its head, and there are plenty of career counselors and self-help books that will steer you in the opposite direction. But what she says makes so much sense. We try on the clothes that we'll wear all day before we buy them. Why don't we try on the work we'll do all day before we commit to it? That's harder to do if you've already drawn up your plan.

III

My first Monday without a job—that one single day—was an emotional roller coaster, and I don't remember ever experiencing one like it before. And I had many, many, *many* more days like that over the course of the next year or so. I still have them sometimes! I catch myself in the "Oh sh*t!" moment, feeling like a failure because I don't have my plan laid out, and I'm still not sure if I have a new identity or what. But then again, I like the way Wendy Harris framed it when we talked, about a year or so into her leap: "You have these days when you're feeling like, I can do it. No I can't. And they're sometimes the same day. I would say, weirdly, in the last month, it has just started that I'm not quite so roller coastery, but instead I feel like this is going to work out. I don't entirely know how. But I love that I can't answer the question, 'Where do you see yourself in five years?' It's a question I don't really want to answer. The answer is, 'I don't know.' And isn't that exciting and fun?"

Yes. Yes, it is. Mostly.

3.
RUNNING
FROM FEAR

The first question I get from most people when they hear I quit my job is "Why did you leave?" The second question is usually "What finally made you do it?" Everybody wants to know what the straw was, and how I got over the fear of the unknown.

It's really hard to describe that final straw without going into the details I've decided not to share about decisions that were being made in the newsroom. But I can tell you about something else that was happening in my life, outside of work, that I think played an important part in my ability to follow my gut when it told me it was time to go. So before we get to the rest of the leap, a very personal story about what contributed to that decision, and my ability, to pull the trigger. Yes, it had to do with issues in my workplace and restlessness with my subject matter. But I also think that the changes I'd already brought upon myself—good ones—gave me a confidence I didn't have before and a belief in my ability to overcome adversities of my own making. I was living the phrase on one of my running shirts that said, "Kickin' Your Ass One Step at a Time."

I mentioned in the first chapter that weight has been an issue for me most of my adult life. I gained twenty pounds my first year in college, and yo-yoed up and down for the next twenty years. That struggle came to a head in August 2011, exactly one year before my leap.

That summer, August of 2011, the United States was in the middle of another financial crisis, this time because of the nation's debt ceiling. It had reached the point that Standard & Poor's had downgraded America's sovereign debt rating. It was the story of the summer, with all manner of financial "experts" predicting a global meltdown if and when the downgrade were to happen. The downgrade happened, and, well, we are all still here.

But Americans were hungry for information about what this downgrade would mean for their own personal finances. All the gloom and doom talk had people scared out of their wits that we were about to go into yet another recession, or even a depression, and that the stock market would tank and they would lose all of their retirement and college savings funds. Again. Thank you, nightly news. I felt like this was a rerun of every other crisis we'd been through over the past five years, and I tried to tell listeners to just keep their money where it was, to hold on for the long haul, and to not futz with it.

A couple of days before I was supposed to leave for a niece's wedding in Massachusetts, CNN called and asked if I would do a segment for one of their morning shows, talking about what people should be doing with their finances in light of the downgrade.

It was an enormous career opportunity. When CNN calls,

you say yes. It doesn't mean you're suddenly going to get a lucrative job in TV, but it does mean visibility for whatever you're doing, including my little weekend radio show. They wanted me to go to a studio in LA for a remote interview with an anchor in Atlanta or New York, I can't remember which.

I said no. I couldn't stomach the idea of being on television. I was overweight, with plenty of that extra Tess showing up in the chubby cheeks on my face. And the camera—I swear!—adds way more than ten pounds. I was so self-conscious about my looks that I never even allowed producers to take photographs of me when we were out in the field on stories for *Marketplace*—photos that would have been destined for the show's website. "There's a reason I'm in radio!" I'd joke while pushing any and all lenses away from my face. So I was already photograph averse, and the idea of being on TV was just beyond what I thought my psyche could deal with. So I made up some excuse (probably along the lines of "I have to clean up the dog poop in the backyard, and it's going to take days!") and I said no to CNN.

A couple of days later, I left for that wedding, and I started beating myself up about the fact that I, alone, was responsible for the fact that I had passed up a big, big, big opportunity. Nobody else was responsible for the fact that I didn't like how I looked and yet I hadn't done anything about it. Nobody else could change that for me. It was all on me.

It was almost all I could think about while we were in Boston. The stakes were very real this time. I had torpedoed something that could further my career just because I didn't like how I looked.

I've never been an athlete, despite being tall (I'm five feet, nine inches). The girls' volleyball and basketball teams nosed around me in high school, but I was more interested in theater and choir and my piano studies. The only physical activity I ever trained for was swimming, and that was short-lived. As an adult, gym memberships came and went, as did kickboxing classes and aerobics studios. I'd usually crap out after a few weeks.

So when it occurred to me to try running, I thought I was bonkers. Someone had told me about an app called Couch-to-5K that promised to turn couch potatoes into runners. I figured it was at least cheap, and all I'd have to do is lace up and get out the front door. I asked my husband if he would commit to getting up early in the morning with me to try this. I knew I wouldn't do it without having someone else to hold me accountable and to set a second alarm. He agreed, and two weeks after we got back from Boston, we downloaded the app and started the program. It was just before Labor Day 2011.

It was ridiculously hard. Even though the program starts you off with mostly walking and just a tiny bit of jogging, I was pretty sure I was going to keel over and Dan would have to call an ambulance about halfway through. But two months later, around Thanksgiving, we found ourselves actually running two and three miles every couple of days. It worked. I couldn't believe it. Coupled with walking the dogs every day for forty-five minutes, my pants started to feel loose.

In January 2012, four months after that first walk-jog, I ran my first 5k, a race around Pasadena's Rose Bowl. The finish line was on the fifty-yard line inside the stadium, and I cried as I crossed it. It was the biggest athletic feat of my then forty-two years. Then in May 2012 I ran my first 10k. And I resolved to run a half marathon by the end of the year.

That kind of change is a victory by anyone's standards.

I was terrified when I started. But I faced that fear through some weird, unexplainable combination of stubbornness, impulsiveness, and exasperation. I just downloaded an app and walked out the front door. The success was gradual, but undeniable, and the results were enough to change the entire way I thought about myself and my self-worth. When you're not shrinking away from who you are, it's a lot easier to imagine the person you might become.

By the time August 2012 rolled around, the month I resigned, I'd lost somewhere north of thirty-five pounds. I'd started wearing bright colors instead of my usual closetful of black and beige. I got a shorter haircut and style to frame my face instead of hiding behind a shoulder-length bob that, I thought, covered up my nonexistent jawline. (The shorter cut also helped hide the fact that my hair was falling out from stress.) People kept telling me how great I looked and how much happier I seemed. And when it came to my physical appearance, it was true. I felt accomplished too, and somehow powerful, because I had taken control of my own physical issues.

I fully believe that the physical change I experienced, and the boosted confidence that accompanied it, played an outsized role in my decision to resign without having something else lined up. A friend told me around that time that when you start getting your body in shape, you generate more testosterone, even as a woman. I have no idea whether that's true, and I haven't been able to find any study that says it is, but it certainly felt like I'd grown some balls that allowed me to say I was mad as hell and wasn't going to take it anymore. I do not believe I would have quit *Marketplace* if I hadn't felt that power of liking myself just a little bit more and if I hadn't believed that I could weather whatever adversity this career decision might throw my way. Maybe the running just made me more willing to take a risk. I don't know. But I'm convinced that it had something to do with my actions in August 2012.

"Change begets change," Dickens wrote in *The Life and Adventures of Martin Chuzzlewit.* "Nothing propagates so fast. If a man habituated to a narrow circle of cares and pleasures, out of which he seldom travels, steps beyond it, though for never so brief a space, his departure from the monotonous scene on which he has been an actor of importance would seem to be the signal for instant confusion."

Or as my friend Aaron McHugh puts it, "There's a 100 percent probability that if you do nothing new, nothing new will come."

I did something new, and all kinds of new came from that point forward.

So if you want to quit but you don't see a way to do it, try changing something else in your life and see where that leads you. You probably even know it already. We all have That Thing—that bad habit, that annoying tendency, that odd compulsion—that we want to change. Start with the small stuff and see where it leads. Malcolm Gladwell writes about this in *The Tipping Point* (which includes plenty of examples of small changes leading to terrible things, but nevertheless!). Charles Duhigg writes about it in *The Power of Habit.* "Small wins are exactly what they sound like. 'Small wins are a steady application of a small advantage,' one Cornell professor wrote in 1984. 'Once a small win has been accomplished, forces are set in motion that favor another small win.' Small wins fuel transformative changes by leveraging tiny advantages into patterns that convince people that bigger achievements are within reach."

I like to think of it as your personal version of the butterfly effect. You flap a small set of wings in one area of your life, and you end up with a hurricane.

As a postscript, I lost a total of forty-six pounds between Labor Day 2011 and the end of 2012. And I did run that half marathon—two weeks before my final day at *Marketplace*. It was like nothing I had ever experienced. I cried again at that finish line, just as I had earlier in the year after my first 5k. It gave me an important victory just before I stepped off the cliff into my leap, where I was *sure* I would have to face defeat. But it gave me both physical and emotional strength that I leaned into in the weeks after leaving my job.

I slowly slacked off the running a few months after I quit my job. I think I had a lot of other emotional issues to tackle, and I got lazy and stopped racing and training. But I carried with me the knowledge that I had faced that fear of the pavement. That has served me each and every time a new opportunity or challenge has come along over the last couple of years. Because if I can run a half marathon—even just one—*and* quit my job at pretty much the same time, that makes it all the harder to imagine what I *can't* do.

4.
THE EAT,
PRAY,
LOVE THING

Those first days and weeks after leaving *Marketplace* boasted one harsh reality after another.

I didn't have anywhere to go in the morning.

I didn't have assignments.

I didn't have colleagues to do a morning Starbucks run for me or me for them.

I didn't have rush-hour traffic (OK, that wasn't a harsh reality; it was a terrific one).

I didn't have a paycheck.

What I did have was a surfeit of self-doubt and fear that my life would never be the same. And more than anything, I felt utterly alone. Not lonely, but just . . . isolated in what I was experiencing. Even though I hadn't been gone any longer than I had been previously for simple vacations, I started to feel as if I was disappearing from the airwaves and on my way to becoming obsolete in my field. It wasn't logical, but without a future planned out for myself, I worried almost immediately that I would never be able to get back to the career heights I'd just left. People would forget about me soon enough, especially once I was replaced on the show I'd hosted. Within days, I started feeling as if I'd lost the only identifying factor about myself—at least the important one. I was still blond. I was still tall. I was still a wife. I was still a resident of Los Angeles. But the really important identifier—"anchor of a national news radio program"—was gone. And it's the only identity I'd known for more than a decade.

In addition, for one of the first times in my adult life, I wasn't busy. I had some work, including short stints backup hosting on radio shows, but not a lot. Suddenly I had time to do all those non-work-related projects that had been languishing on the back burner. I'd mentally allotted myself a month to just relax and do nothing—hey, after twenty years of working constantly, I had earned it! I could have read the dozen or so books that were sitting, unopened, on my iPad. I could have started practicing the piano again. I could have finally cleared out both the attic and garage of all the clutter that had accumulated over the years. I could have torn up the grass in the backyard with my own hands and replaced it with drought-tolerant landscaping!

But I couldn't relax, because I was worried about Everything in the World, and I couldn't get my butt in gear. Now instead of being worried and anxious and stressed about the job that I did have, I was worried and anxious and stressed about the one that I didn't have. All I could do was look backward and wonder if I had just done the dumbest thing *ever.* I didn't really tell anyone except my husband how awful I was feeling. As far as friends knew, I was a happy camper because, oh, man, did they wish they could do the same thing! Anyone with a steady job would be quick to say he or she would love the opportunity to sleep until the afternoon. But when you're in the stew after quitting, it doesn't feel like a luxury. It feels lazy. It feels like there's something wrong with you.

I'd heard about this feeling before, in almost every interview I'd ever done with someone who'd been laid off. The difference in my case, of course, was that I hadn't been laid off. I left entirely of my own accord, and I had no one to blame but myself for every bad feeling I was having. I didn't feel like I could complain about my worries and fears to anyone else, because I had brought this on myself. What are you prattling on about? You wanted this; otherwise, you shouldn't have done it!

"This is so great for you to have a vacation. Well deserved!"

"I can't believe how lucky you are to be able to just walk away."

"You're doing what the rest of us dream of doing. Taking a break. That's awesome."

Those are from actual e-mails I received after leaving my job. People automatically assume you are taking a break, because no one in his or her right mind just up and quits without a backup plan. You must be taking time to find yourself or whatever, because what else would you be doing?

"Lisa" wrote to me in mid-2014, saying she'd just left her twenty-five-year career in technology. She said it wasn't her dream job, but I'd say twenty-five years qualifies as a fully formed career.

"People have congratulated me on 'a well-deserved vacation.' But it's certainly not a vacation as some of my friends seem to think."

Ah, yes, we have our own little club, don't we.

I shouldn't have cared what anybody else thought I was doing. But I did. I was absurdly concerned with what other people would think of me. I wanted people to be throwing new job offers my way, and I worried that all of those people who could have been doing that figured I already had a plan. I wondered if well-meaning friends who expressed confidence that the Next Great Thing would come along secretly thought I was lazy, reckless, and entitled. That may be because *I* thought, more than once, that I was lazy, reckless, and entitled. I figured most people would think I was on the express train to crazytown (which even I started to believe). Or they'd assume I had three years' worth of savings in the bank (I should have, being the host of a personal finance show, but I didn't—more on that later). Or they would assume that my husband made enough to support both of us and my income was just gravy.

Some people I knew joked that since I didn't do it after graduating from college, maybe this was my time to go backpacking and stay in hostels across Europe. A few wondered if I might go back to school and get a master's degree, or try cooking school because I love giving dinner parties and spending time in the kitchen. There was an assumption that this was a break from it all, a chance to have fun and just live life without a daily grind for a while.

If only.

III

Margie Weinstein calls all this the "eat, pray, love thing."

She's a Manhattanite who had what anyone would consider

a cool job. For almost ten years she worked at the Whitney Museum, several of those years in charge of education programs for what is without question one of this country's great art institutions. When she up and quit without knowing what she wanted to do next, she says people assumed she was just doing her "eat, pray, love thing"—because anyone without a plan (especially a woman without a plan) must be looking to travel to exotic locales and take lovers and . . . eat.

Ah yes, the eat, pray, love thing. I could relate to that. People said that to me, too, only half-jokingly. And it was annoying. I'm all for taking that kind of journey if you can, if you have the money, if you are willing and able to walk away from responsibilities and relationships. If that's the path for you, then go for it. But everyone assumed that a trip around the world to find your true self was the one thing that made sense about just up and leaving a job without having a plan. And that was far too pat and oversimplified. That's not to say it wouldn't have been fun, and maybe even fulfilling, but it's just not realistic for most people. Including me. And I didn't want people to think that's what I was doing, because then people would definitely stop thinking of me as an accomplished career woman who wanted to stay in the game, even if she wasn't sure what that game was.

Margie loved her job right up until her last day of work. "Basically I was creating public programs for the Whitney, in consultation with the curators, thinking about, 'All right, what are the programs that the Whitney should present in conjunction with these exhibitions?' And then coming up with panelists and programs and artists, and then making it all happen. I loved the artists; I loved my colleagues; I loved what I did.

And it was really a dream job. It was also a job that was— and this isn't how I measured success—very much coveted by other people. In fact, it is probably the type of job that, as soon as you told people who you were, they would say something like, 'I'd love to have that job. That must be so great.' I felt incredibly lucky. And it's not even just in hindsight or nostalgia. I really felt proud of it and thought it was really meaningful, and I never, ever took it for granted."

Lots of factors went into her decision to leave. The Whitney was in the midst of a move to a different part of Manhattan, and as part of that process, the job she was in was likely going to need her to stick around and see through the transition for several years. That transition was happening at a time when she was debating whether she wanted to do museum work for her entire career. On top of that, she'd always been interested in the subject of income inequality, and as she looked around at an economy in shambles post-2008 financial crisis, she wanted to explore whether she could help make a difference on that front by getting involved in politics. "At various times I'd actually made off-the-cuff jokes about it. Like in 2004 I said, 'That's it, I'm getting out and going into politics!' And in 2008 I said, 'That's it, I'm leaving and I'm going into politics!' So people had been hearing me say these little things throughout the years. I wanted to move into progressive social change work."

In 2013 Margie gave six months' notice. She told friends who expressed surprise at her plan to depart without another job in place that those six months would be her time to search and network and do all the things you're supposed to do, including informational interviews. In reality, though, she was too busy working those final months at the Whitney to look for work—something I had definitely experienced and that a lot of the people I spoke to did too. So when she left, she didn't have a job, and she had no idea what would come next.

When I met up with her in New York City in early 2014, she had been away from the Whitney for about eight months.

"It's been up and down. Mostly good. I read about someone who had made a comparison between being content and being happy and who said, you know, happiness sort of goes up and down, but you can be generally content. And that made a lot of sense to me. But there definitely have been moments when I have doubted myself or really felt like, you know, What is going to happen to me? What if this really drags on for much longer than I expected? What will become of me? I've never regretted my decision, and I feel like that's the true test, but I have likened it to a divorce in the sense that even if it's your choice, it can still be really difficult."

I think the comparison between this process and a divorce is pretty accurate, even though, like Margie, I have no personal experience with the latter. Quitting a long-term job, a success-ful career, is a relationship split, and it has many of the same emotional and psychological difficulties. It's also something that's hard to explain to other people, who never know what to say to you anyway. Margie told me that one of the hardest parts of the transition was coming up with the elevator pitch to explain her situation to others, especially those who assumed she was getting ready for her "eat, pray, love trip." "I cannot tell you the number of people who have asked me, 'What do your days actually look like? What do you do during the day?'"

I got that question all the time too, and I loathed it (though at least I could tell people I was writing a book—which didn't help dispel the "eat, pray, love idea").

But when it came to figuring out what the days would

actually look like, the best piece of advice I've heard is something that Margie's friend told her. Margie described her conversation with her friend this way:

"I was thinking about filling my day, and I was saying that, OK, I'm going to get up, go to the gym, and I'll go to the New York Public Library, which is where I had gone to write my dissertation, and I love it. I love libraries, super-pro libraries, and I particularly love the New York Public Library on Forty-Second Street because it's just physically beautiful. And, you know, I'll bring my laptop. They open at 10 a.m., they close at 5 p.m., and I'll be there from ten to five. It will be just like a workday. I'll pack my lunch, and I'll just search for a job from there, and then I'll feel like I'm really working.

"My friend just sort of looked at me, in the best possible way, as if I were crazy, and she asked, 'Why would you do that? Why would you put in a full day as if you were working? There are only so many jobs out there, and you have to wait for people to get back to you anyway with the informational interviews. Why don't you just work in the morning and give yourself the afternoon off to read a book or go to a museum, because you'll never have this time again?'

"And I said, 'You are so right!' And so I have taken her advice. Most days I spend the morning working, and then many afternoons I have gone to museums or I have spent the afternoon reading."

I love that advice. If you're making a leap, *take that advice.* Structure your day and your schedule so that you *can.* Why not take advantage of that time? It's a way to give yourself the full stop that you might have been craving before you quit. Or maybe you didn't even know you were craving it. But we can all benefit from having time to rejuvenate, to have experiences that might even end up holding guilt at bay—guilt for having leapt in the first place. If you're getting off the hamster wheel, even for a limited period of time, you might as well take full advantage of it, because the likelihood is small that you'll allow yourself that kind of time again.

Margie also told me that she'd come to realize that people's reaction to her departure, and what she'd done afterward, was more a reflection of them than of her and that the people who expressed deep, deep anxiety about it probably have deep, deep anxiety about their own careers. "And so I am now better able to gauge people's response," she said. "If they say, 'Wow, but don't you feel really unproductive?' that's really much more about them than the fact that I actually am by some metric unproductive."

That is *such* a healthy way to go about this transition time. I wish I hadn't spent so much time feeling guilty every time I just ditched the freelance thing for a few hours—or a couple of days!—and went out and had fun. I wish I had taken the time to rejuvenate instead. If I had it to do all over again, I would set aside time each day, or bigger chunks each week, to do things I wouldn't be able to do if I still had a nine-to-five job. Even if that meant taking naps or sitting in the garden! You shouldn't feel guilty about having some time to be unproductive—unstructured time is great for creativity and inspiration. Guilt should not stop you from enjoying the time off that you risked so much to take. That said, you shouldn't be spending all day in your pajamas. You need to look for ways to enrich your life so that you rediscover your identity outside of your job (more on this later). If individuals or part of your community frown upon your free time, I say that's just because everybody else wants to have free time too. And who the hell cares what anybody else thinks anyway?

Oh, right. I do.

III

I worried so much about what my actions would mean for the people around me and what they would think of me for abandoning my post, so to speak. The day I decided that I needed to quit, I sat for three hours in my backyard, waiting for my husband to get home, and I could not figure out how to tell him that I wanted to jump ship. And not just wanted to, but had to. I basically blurted it out as soon as he walked down the stairs to the patio: "I can't do this anymore. I'm done."

He didn't miss a beat. I'm not exaggerating—he looked at me sobbing in our cushy outdoor chairs, and he immediately said, "OK, we'll make it work." Just like that. I started to apologize and try to explain myself, and he just said something like, "Look, this isn't a surprise to me. You've needed to do this, and maybe, sure, it would be easier if you had another job lined up, but you have to do this."

I was a wreck, and I couldn't understand why he wasn't. But he just wasn't fazed. We had smaller conversations for a few days after that, leading up to my handing in my resignation letter, but he never expressed anything but support and confidence in my decision.

Loyalty trumps realism in many relationships, which can be both good and bad. When you're in a place that is this vulnerable, it's easy to stop trusting not only your *own* judgment, but everyone else's too—husband, best friend, mother, father, mentor, colleague. Hearing nothing but blanket support feels even more isolating, because you just assume that everyone feels bad for you and won't be honest in their appraisal of your situation. Your loved ones will tell you that you need to do what's best for you and that they have faith that it will work out in the end. But sometimes you don't need support. You need a strategy. And to get that, I was surprised by how hard you have to push that conversation, especially with those closest to you, to see if you can get beyond the Happy Talk, as well intentioned as it might be. One of the biggest laugh lines from my World Domination Summit speech was this:

What's amazing about a leap of faith is how everyone around you is so sure it's gonna work out.

When I wrote it, I wasn't thinking of it as a laugh line. For me, it was more of a lament. I wanted to talk to everyone about how scared I was; how much I regretted my own choices; how stupid I felt. But it's impossible to do that when they're all telling you that this is going to be the best thing you ever did in your whole life and that your Next Thing is going to be even bigger than the last. Happy Talk—that thing where your friends and family will back you up onehundredpercent nomatterwhateveniftheythinkyou'renuts—is what you do as a friend, spouse, mother, father, brother, or sister when someone you love makes a big change. But a big part of me wanted someone to step up and say, "Yeah, you're an idiot, and this is the biggest mistake of your life." Because at least with that person, I wouldn't wonder what he or she was *really* thinking.

That said, I would learn over the months that followed that the real issue was mine—I *didn't* have the confidence that I'd find my way through. My husband did. And so did many people around me. They didn't see my decision as any sort of failure, even though I did. They honestly believed I would be fine, even though I didn't. And it took me a long time to accept that any of it was anything other than Happy Talk, meant to boost me up while I was down and out and floundering for answers.

III

For Candysse Miller, it wasn't a cakewalk explaining her leap to her father. She was thirty years into a successful career, much of it as an executive director for an insurance association. When she left, she wanted to go into independent publishing and winemaking, but she didn't have it all lined up before giving notice.

"Dad was terrified for me," she said. "Just the thought that there was any uncertainty with my career frightened him. He's old-school—you know, two main jobs over the course of an entire career, . . . and he was in his eighties. I think I actually submitted my letter of resignation before I told my dad, but I'd warmed him up and kind of let him know I was thinking about this. He was mortified. 'You can't leave without another job!' Well, finally I caught him on a day when I knew he was feeling good, he was in good spirits, and I said, 'Dad, I did it.' I said, 'Here's my game plan, and I'm really enthusiastic.' Of course, the first thing he said was, 'What if those don't work out?' I told him, 'Well, one, I've got a plan. I'm collaborating with people who are successful in their own right in these different fields. I know there's no one in the world I'll work harder for than myself.' And I said, 'Here's what I've got in the bank, and I know it's entirely possible that I will not have an income for an entire year. I've got enough to see me through for a few years here if need be. I don't want it to be that, but I'm going to be OK.' And by the end of the conversation, I'm not going to say he was on board with it, but he was accepting of it."

I think it's so wonderful how she sat her dad down and had this honest conversation about his fears and how she responded to them. She was confident in her decision and had specific answers for the questions she knew her dad would raise. (I was a blubbering mess when I told my parents I was quitting.) She also didn't expect her father to be 100 percent OK with her decision. She just wanted him to understand her reasoning behind it. And now her dad is her biggest advocate.

"The interesting thing," she said, "is that just in the last week, we were talking about it over breakfast, and he said, 'Don't get down about any of this, because you are going to be a success at this, I just know it, because you're doing everything right.' I thought that was just the highest endorsement I could possibly get." She knew he wouldn't sugarcoat his thoughts, and here he was expressing more confidence in her than she even had in herself. This is when you let your loved ones be strong on your behalf. It's remarkable to realize that the people in your life believe what you're doing is a good option. It feels so wonderful to know that they understand you're not just living out an "eat, pray, love" cliché.

III

I spent a lot of time after I left *Marketplace* obsessing over whether people would think I had lost all my ambition. I wondered if they'd think I was no longer successful because I didn't have a brand name (*Marketplace*! NPR!) attached to my name. As I've noted, I was inordinately preoccupied with what everybody else thought and how my leap looked from the outside.

My parents, though? I knew they loved me. I knew they would want only whatever was best for me. And I knew they would support me in any decision I made. They're my parents—that's their job, and they do it well. When I called and told them that August afternoon that I thought it was finally time to pull the ripcord at *Marketplace*, they immediately said exactly what I thought they would: "We support whatever you feel you need to do. But are you sure? You love this job!" Sure, you've had hardships, they said, like everyone does at their workplace, but you've always seemed so happy with the work itself. And they were right. They went on to say that no matter what my decision, they supported it, and me, and they had exactly zero doubt that I'd find the next great opportunity for myself. "You're the only one who can decide what's best for you," my dad said, "and you're smart and you're driven and you'll have no trouble at all." My mom just kept telling me how much they loved me and how she understood why I was leaving. She'd been on the receiving end of plenty of calls at the end of particularly exasperating days I'd had at work.

Mom and Dad said all the right things, but deep inside my psyche I didn't believe them. I just *knew* that they thought I was making the biggest mistake of my life, but because they were my parents, they were obligated to say otherwise. I just *knew* that they were disappointed in me. I just *knew* that they were worried out of their skulls about my well-being. And our bank account. I'd been successful from the get-go, even as a child, and now I was a "quitter."

My parents are easily the greatest influences on my life. They will have celebrated their fiftieth wedding anniversary in August 2015. They're both in their early seventies, healthy, and leading adventurous lives. They've traveled the globe over the last decade or so. Dad still works as a surgeon at the VA hospital in Portland, and Mom is a professional, though volunteer, advocate and fund-raiser for nonprofit organizations, including her current service as chair of the Oregon Arts Commission.

It's safe to say that a driving force in my life has been to show the world that my parents did a bang-up job with me. I know my parents would have been proud of me no matter what career I ended up in. But one of the great joys of being on the national airwaves was that every once in a while they got to share in the cool factor of it all. For the past twenty years, Mom has called or (since the late nineties) e-mailed to tell me when people, often strangers, recognized her last name and asked if she was related to me. She has shared these moments with me first and foremost because she knows they'll make *me* feel special, but I've always thought and hoped that she takes a little personal delight in being a part of those small slices of the (very) modest fame I achieved. I have thought and hoped that it tickled both of them to have that association, to know that their daughter's success has been a public success and to have a little of that fairy dust settle on them as well.

Having my own radio show made me part of an exclusive club, and for me that felt like the fulfillment of How Things Were Supposed to Be. Throughout my childhood and young adulthood, I'd been told how remarkable I was and how I had an extraordinary future ahead of me. My mother has reminded me several times over the years that I started talking when I was nine months old. I excelled as a musician from my first piano lessons at age five. I excelled as a student. I skipped a grade and went to a top university at age seventeen. I got a high-profile job six weeks after graduating. Four years later I got a better job, and I got a more lucrative job another three years after that. By age thirty-two I was one of the hosts of a national radio program. Five years later I got my own show. I worked hard for all of it, but I also felt destined for it because of the way I had been raised and the path I had been set on from a fairly early age. In some ways, it all came very easily to me, which made it less of a challenge to live up to the expectations.

All of which is to say that one thing I've always wanted to avoid is disappointing the two people who had worked so hard to build me up into the confident and driven woman that I am. Deciding to be unemployed, voluntarily? That's not something you relish telling your parents. I was convinced for months that my parents must have been thinking I was nuts and that I was throwing away the career that they helped nurture. I knew they still loved me, but I thought that they had to be disappointed in the fact that I couldn't just stick it out like a grown-up.

So more than a year after the leap, I sat them down at their home in Portland and asked them—*really* asked them—about their reactions when I quit.

"My reaction?" my dad asked. "I had no worries. Because I knew you'd find something else that you would enjoy."

"You didn't worry about the fact that I wasn't going to have an income?"

"No."

"Dad, come on. Really?"

"No," he told me. "Absolutely not. Because I knew it was short term and that you could do whatever you wanted to do."

"How did you know it was short term? *I* didn't know it was going to be short term."

"Because I didn't think you were ready to just stay home."

"And retire!" Mom jumped in.

Dad laughed. "And retire."

"But," I insisted, "there was no guarantee that I was going to get another job."

"Well, only about a ninety-nine percent guarantee," said Dad. "Because people with talent and a background like yours are going to get a job. One way or another, somewhere. I had no concerns about your getting another job if that's what you wanted to do."

"You didn't think I was crazy for not having something else lined up before I left?"

"No, but there again, it's about self-confidence and confidence in the world around you. It's risky when you quit a job and you don't have another job lined up. I think the risk of just being around and not having things to do are the biggest risks. Economically, we did not worry. I had total confidence, and I didn't lose a minute's sleep over it."

I turned to my mother. "Did you?"

"No," she said, "because I did know everything that was going on at work. And for you to be so unhappy, that was the worst thing that could happen. But, no, I really didn't worry.

The fact that you did it took a lot of guts. And knowing the situation, I think you did the right thing."

"It was a big move," Dad added, "and that kind of a change has got to be really difficult. But if you're unhappy, I think it's imperative. You've got a lot of life to live, and you don't want to live it being unhappy eight or ten hours a day, five days a week."

I told them I was surprised, given the generation they're from, that they were so sanguine about all of it. People their age grew up in a world where you got a job and then you were in that job for forty years and you retired. So I figured for them, what I did would seem unorthodox and, frankly, a little weird. Dad reminded me that the other major generational change is the two-income family. "If you have two wage earners," he said, "then the risk of one of them stopping work and changing careers can be much more manageable than it is when you're the only breadwinner. So that's a huge difference."

Mom wrapped it all up in a bow. "I guess I also like to think that we have evolved as two older people, enough to not say, 'Well, because this was the way we did it, this is the way you should do it.' So I guess I just have to tell you very honestly, it never crossed my mind to say, 'She shouldn't be quitting a job because, well, she just shouldn't be quitting a job.' This isn't about anybody else in the entire world. This is about our daughter. This is about you and what makes you happy. And it's your life. It's got to be what makes you want to get up in the morning and go to work. What makes you happy when you come home at night and want to go to the next day. For you to be happy is what matters for us. And that's just the bottom line."

At that point, I cried. And through the tears I asked one final question: "Well, what if I decide to go work at Starbucks?"

"Perfect," said Dad. "You're a people person. You could interview all of them. You'd probably have more interesting stories than you've ever had."

"But I'm supposed to continue to do remarkable things. What if I don't?"

"Then you rest on your laurels, and you enjoy what you've done, and you're proud of it, and you're comfortable with it. There are people every day who leave successful careers and retire. You've accomplished a ton."

And finally . . . I believed them. I really, truly believed them. I knew they still hoped that I would find that next great thing for myself—what parent wouldn't?—but I also knew that there was no disappointment in me, no sense that I'd done something from which I could never recover. And once I believed that my parents felt that way, it was much easier for me to feel that way. This total belief that I would land on my feet was probably the same belief they had in me that enabled me to succeed in the first place. Everybody needs to feel self-confident in order to survive this kind of leap, but they also have to feel the confidence of those around them. Identify who those people are in your life and talk with them immediately and often. And make sure to talk with them when the self-doubt starts to creep in so that you can get yourself back on track.

|||

Although leaping is a decision only you can make—along with immediate family—the people you surround yourself with, especially at work, can have a significant effect on your decision-making process. They can even play a role in your "inability" to leap and to change. I already mentioned Herminia Ibarra's exhortation to actively work toward a new career identity. Her second piece of advice is to tweak your network, surround yourself with new people. "The people that you're close to already think that they know you," she told me, "but they know you in the past, who you've been. Whereas you are, in your head, imagining yourself in the future. So there's a gap there. Because they can't really share that, and you're unstable and confused if you're in the middle of all this, they're scared of what you might do to your career, to the family unit, to the workplace, that you're going to upset an equilibrium that has already been set. It could be a coworker who's older who had the opportunity to change and chose not to. It could be a partner who sees his or her revenue halved by the situation. It could be any number of things. But change upsets what has already been established, and so people can be very conservative." All of which is understandable and to be expected. But it means you must broaden your circle of advisers and expose yourself to people who do not work with you, or even in your industry.

All kinds of people have approached me after hearing of my leap, asking for advice on how to do it themselves, but none more so than my public radio colleagues across the country. Many of them cannot imagine doing what I did. It is an extraordinarily insular industry, and it's one that many people have trouble leaving, even if they're under poor management or other negative circumstances, purely because of its external cachet. Tell colleagues at your large-market public station that you want to leave and they'll respond with, "But what else *is* there?" And you, of course, say, "Oh, you're right. I couldn't possibly leave, because I'm lucky to work at this place that so many people love! Except me!"

Find other voices. "The people who know us best," Ibarra wrote in a paper, "may wish to be supportive, but they tend to reinforce—or even desperately try to preserve—the old identities we are trying to shed." She also cautions against relying on career counselors who "are in the business of facilitating incremental moves along an established trajectory."

As you're trying on those new work identities, experimenting with what other career paths you might leap to, don't forget to find people who are already on those paths and make them your new BFFs. Or at least coffee buddies!

III

One other valuable lesson I learned from Margie Weinstein is that misery (and uncertainty) loves company. When you're in the soup of wondering what people are thinking about you and your decision to get off the track, it can be enormously helpful to hang with other people who've done the same.

A couple of months into her leap, Margie found out that some other friends and acquaintances had made their own recent leaps. They all started to have regular dinners together, and ultimately they decided to call themselves the North Stars, because they were all looking for their career North Star. Wendy Harris is one too. They met (and still meet!) every two weeks to share stories of the job hunt and to talk about the experience of living in the leap. I joined them one evening in

New York and marveled at the commonalities in our experiences.

One of the Stars, Kate (she asked me not to use her last name), talked about other people, wondering how she could make a leap midcareer when she was already established in her industry. "The idea that it's too late to do or learn something new is soul-sucking," she said. She also noted that, particularly in the first few weeks after departing her job, she had a "dark moment of the soul" when she not only felt bad about her career search but also about how she looked, the non-work clothes she was wearing, and more. And it's true. Going from office attire to jeans and a T-shirt feels like you're almost giving up on yourself and your appearance. It's something entrepreneurs and stay-at-home parents have to come to grips with. There are two ways to deal with it: (1) dress the way you did at work, though most professionals would rather not, or (2) embrace it. Embrace your inner slob and get comfortable. (And remember how much money you're saving because you're not buying clothes!)

"I think when you've had some success," said Wendy, "the hardest thing is to turn off what other people think about you. I could not turn off the 'Well, if I do this, people will think I failed. Or if I do that, people will think that I'm not smart.' I still struggle with that."

Yes, yes, and yes. Just about everyone I talked to echoed Wendy's struggle, no matter what kind of job they'd held and whether it had a cool factor or not. We glean so much self-worth from our careers and our jobs that it can be really difficult to opt out of that when it feels like other people have defined your success for you. And it's really hard to redefine that for yourself. "Success has to be being happy," Wendy said. "It can't just be money. It can't just be that people think you're smart. It has to be that you get some satisfaction out of what you do. And that means different things for different people. Someone once told me that he saw somebody who used to be a client, someone we both knew, and that person asked, 'How's Wendy doing? Is she doing OK?' This former client had thought I'd been let go. Because no one would choose to do this. And that sent me into a tailspin that it should not have. And I kept saying to myself, 'Don't let it bother you.' But it really did. It bothered me a lot. There are things like that that come up, when you're feeling like people are judging you. I can't say that I don't care what people think, but I care a lot less, because on a day-to-day basis, I'm really enjoying life. If you ask me, 'Who's successful?' I'm still pretty good!"

I felt as if I'd found my spirit animals with this group, and it made me wish I had a group like this back in California. If you're thinking about quitting, you could do much worse than getting your own constellation of North Stars.

III

Here's something I'd love to see happen: go to a party and have your work be the very last thing anyone asks you about. Of course, when I was a national journalist, it was the first thing I wanted to tell everybody! Now, I don't really have an answer.

Think back to the last time you met someone new. Maybe it was at a bar. Maybe you were in a class. Maybe you were at a party, standing by the food and not wanting anyone to come up to you because you're terrible with small talk, but, oh, crap, here comes somebody: "Hi! I'm Kathy!"

"Hi, I'm Tess. Nice to meet you."

"So what do you do?"

I used to hope that this question would be the first thing someone asked me, assuming she didn't already recognize me, as most people should, by the mellifluous, dulcet tones emanating from my throat. If the person didn't recognize me, I was always happy to say, "Oh, I'm a journalist."

Cool factor check mark number 1.

"Oh? Do you write for the newspapers?"

"No, I do radio."

Cool factor check mark number 2.

"Really?! Are you actually *on* the radio? Have I heard you?"

"You might have. I'm in public radio."

Cool factor check mark number 3.

"I *love* public radio! Do you know Carl Kasell?"

"No, I don't know him personally, though I'm a fan too. I work on a business news program called *Marketplace*."

"I *love* that show! Do you work with Kai Ryssdal?"

"I do indeed. In fact, we started there within two months of each other back in 2001. His office is down the hall from mine. He has a corner."

"I *love* him! Would I know your name? Wait . . . did you say your name was Tess?"

"Tess Vigeland, yes." (Inner self beams with pride and self-importance. I love listeners.)

"I've totally heard you. I *love* you!"

Awww shucks, thanks.

"You don't look anything like I thought you would." Full stop.

If I'm being honest, those moments were manna for me. I relished them the way I relish an earthy pinot noir from Oregon's Willamette Valley, and I was always more than happy to answer the question "What do you do?" In fact, sometimes, if it didn't enter the conversation right away, I would steer it so that it would. That sounds horribly self-centered and egotistical when I write it, but it's true, and I'd bet I'm not alone in doing so. When you have a great job, a job with a high cool factor, you want people to know it. You want people to ask the question so that you can say ever-so-nonchalantly, "Oh, I'm on the radio."

I'm not the only one who thinks that way. After Jill Abramson was fired by the *New York Times* in 2014, she told *Cosmopolitan* magazine:

"It can be a danger to define yourself by your job. I miss my colleagues and the substance of my work, but I don't miss saying, 'Jill Abramson, executive editor.' I don't. I was once told that a former executive editor of the *Times*, who knew he was going to stop being editor, made sure to make reservations at a particular restaurant because he was afraid after that, they wouldn't give him a table anymore. That's not high on my priority list!'"

I was never famous enough to get tables at fancy restaurants, but if I had been, I probably would have done the same thing that editor did. But good for Jill Abramson!

When you no longer have the cool answer, you dread the question about what you do for work. You try to avoid it. I think that's magnified if you've been a public figure, because then the perceived fall from cool seems so much more dramatic.

In fact, for almost a year, when people would ask, I would reply by saying, "Well, I used to be . . ." And I'd absorb the looks of approval and wonder. And then I'd smile and say yes when they asked if I knew Scott Simon or Robert Siegel.

But then the follow up: "So what are you doing now?"

That question, I didn't want to answer it. I felt shame. I feared being judged. I no longer had something cool to say. It felt like failure, even though the decision had been all my own.

"I'm a freelancer." Look of pity.

"I'm a solo-preneur building a career of writing, voiceover, and event hosting." Look of bewilderment.

"I'm on a break from office life." Oh—so you're unemployed and looking for work? Sorry to hear it.

"I left my twenty-year career and don't know what comes next." Did you win the lottery or something? Aren't you bored? Did you lose your ambition somewhere on the way to the loo?

Most people cannot fathom the idea of leaving a career without having a next step lined up. So the quizzical looks stem from a very real sense that either you've given up on yourself or there's something wrong with your mental or physical health. Explaining it can be exhausting, because everyone wants to know why you left, how you're going to support yourself, what your family said about all of it ... and the whole time your own psyche is revisiting all those same questions that you had banished before this event.

Why *is* this the first question we ask? Why is our work the most important thing people want to know about us?

I now make a point of asking some other question—*any* other question—when I first meet someone. Some of the questions I now ask are these:

- What's your favorite thing to do in this city?
- What kind of travel do you enjoy? When's the last time you did that and where did you go?
- What's your favorite part of the weekend?

Sometimes it feels a little bit weird, and I will literally say to the person I'm just meeting that I hate asking about people's work right off the bat, so I try to ask different questions instead. Most folks appreciate that and return the favor by asking me questions unrelated to my work.

That's what happens in many other countries. In fact, in some places it's considered rude to ask about someone's work until you get to know him. I like that.

We are not our work. Let's stop making that the first thing we want to know about our fellow humans.

5.
WHAT'S
STOPPING YOU?

If there's one refrain that bounced around my head for months after leaving *Marketplace*, it's this: You are officially a quitter. Quitter quitter quitter.

Quit is a four-letter word in this country, not just literally but figuratively as well. If I asked you to tell me the first thing that pops into your head when I say the word *quitter,* I'd bet good money that a lot of you would answer with "Winners never quit, and quitters never win." Even the aphorism itself will not quit in its circular logic. Unless you're quitting some vice like alcohol or smoking, in which case quitters are seen as heroic, quitting is against the American ethos. Quitting = bad. Quitting = weak. Quitting = loser. You never, ever give up. You never, ever quit.

There's a social stigma attached to it that makes the experience of quitting difficult and scary. You just know you will be judged as a failure and that people will think you just can't handle things, that you need to grow up, that you need to grow a pair. And success just magnifies all of it, adding an extra layer of disbelief from those who can't imagine that *you,* with all those accolades and accomplishments, would quit. Surely, you're better than that.

This is why so many of my conversations in the late summer and fall of 2012 went something like this:

So I hear you're leaving Marketplace*!*

Yes I am!

And where are you off to next?

I don't know.

What do you mean?

I don't know. I don't have another job. I just quit.

You what?

I quit.

But aren't there lots of opportunities out there for someone with your skills and experience?

Yes, there probably are.

Then why did you quit? Isn't that a really bad idea? What's wrong with you?

OK, that last part never happened—but I could tell from the way some people looked at me that I might as well have been speaking a foreign language. Nobody in his or her right mind quits, so clearly there was some deeper issue going on with me, because I was too smart to do this.

Peg Streep has been researching quitters—and the process of quitting—for years. She coauthored the book *Mastering the Art of Quitting: Why It Matters in Life, Love, and Work.* I had the chance to meet her a couple of months into my own leap, when the two of us were the featured guests on a talk show about quitting. Before then, I had no idea there is an art to quitting.

In her book, Peg says quitting is "a healthy, adaptive response when a goal can't be reached or what appeared to be a life path turns out to be a blind alley or when life otherwise throws you a curve ball. Simply putting quitting on the table—seeing it as a possible plan of action—is a helpful corrective to the tunnel vision that persistence often creates and a necessary first step toward changing your perspective."

That all makes total sense. For me, it wasn't a blind alley or a curve ball. It was realizing that I would not be able to reach my goal where I was and that it wasn't worth it to stay in that environment if it wasn't going to be a stepping-stone. But what I didn't do was use that realization to spur a plan of action. I didn't *have* a plan of action. But I like Peg's definition of quitting because it reframes what quitting is.

It argues that more of us should quit more often because it would be better for us if we did.

I asked Peg to evaluate my own quitting decision and experience. I admitted to her that I hadn't really told the full story about why I quit, how I quit, and what had happened since I quit. As far as everybody knew, my new life was going just swimmingly. I had lots of freelance jobs, I was all over social media talking about these new opportunities I was exploring with my newfound career freedom, and, oh, by the way, I'm back on the radio, on the other side of the microphone, answering questions about what it's like to leap. Cool! It's all good!

Except it wasn't. I told Peg that actually I had quit in something of a fit of pique (even though I gave three months' notice), that I'd quietly slunk out of the office on my last day, and that since then I'd been alternately overjoyed and paralyzed with panic at what my life looked like without a job to go to every morning. "Oh," she said, "OK, maybe you weren't a good quitter. At least not right away.

"Where you appear to have failed, and where most people fail, is not anticipating how you will react to the free fall," she explained over breakfast. "You didn't recognize that quitting something that was so central to your self-definition would be basically like jumping off a cliff and free-falling." She's right about that. Nobody tells you how much time you're going to spend doubting your own sanity! Or, if I can't blame other people for it, I guess I just didn't bother thinking through what it would feel like to suddenly have my life change so radically, even at my own behest. "It may be at some level that no one would quit anything, ever, if they were realistic," she continued. "The reality of it is that we are all hardwired to persist rather than move on."

In my job in personal finance, I reported on dozens of studies that showed this in the financial world. It's best summed up by Warren Buffett's famous adage, "Be fearful when others are greedy and greedy when others are fearful." It's the primary argument for investing more as the stock market is going down. It's the opposite of what the herd is doing, and it feels like much more of a risk, and yet you're getting stocks while they're cheaper—investments you can ride as the market recovers. It's how smart investors made money after the crash of March 2009, when the Dow hit 6,500. Most people were fearful and selling, meaning that most people were losing all the gains they'd had. Meanwhile, the smart investors piled in while stocks were cheap, and they rode the recovery all the way to riches.

But despite plenty of stories about how going against the

grain can be a smart move, it's still incredibly hard. A study released in April 2014 by behavioral economists at Caltech and Virginia Tech showed that going against what everybody else is doing is much tougher than you'd think, and people who do it actually have something different going on in their brains. They are wired differently. The insular cortex of their brains, which is key in detecting risk, was more active than other people's.[1] Those investors who sold as the market was rising had what the researchers called an "early warning signal" that went off in their brains, and they were uniquely able to pay attention to it, even though everybody else was doing the opposite.

So if we are risk averse in our DNA, and if we have a brain that makes it tougher to go against the norm, it is certainly against our nature to quit, even if quitting is in our best interest.

III

Going against the grain isn't the only reason that it can be hard for people to quit. My public radio colleague Courtenay Hameister wrote a beautiful column in the *Oregon Humanities* magazine in the spring of 2014[2] about leaving her role as the host of a variety show called *Live Wire*. It touched on so many of the same emotions I'd been through after leaving *my* radio show: "There were lots of great reasons to stay, but there remained a dark one: the nagging, terrifying idea that this job was the most interesting thing about me. Once I'd made the mistake of allowing my job to define me in that way, I could no longer consider quitting my job without feeling like I was quitting myself," she wrote. A panic attack just before a live stage show prompted her to finally say "Enough!" But not without the persistent feeling that quitting was going to spell something bad for her notions of who she was.

"The cultural portrait of the quitter—that never-will-amount-to-anything person who lacks staying power—still looms large," Peg Streep writes. And that's something that has seeped into your subconscious whether you realize it or not. Even if everybody else tells you you're brave, you have absorbed the notion, over a lifetime of hearing it, that quitters are losers. It's not true, but it will haunt you unless you actively push that thought away."

Courtenay is a few years younger than I am, but I think she still grew up in a generation in which you were expected to stay in jobs for several years at a stretch and to stick it out even if things started to go sideways. In that way of thinking, *not* quitting shows fortitude, it shows loyalty, and it shows that you are able to rise above whatever difficulties you might be facing. Quitting means you've given up, both on the situation and on your own ability to deal with it. No matter how painful it can be to stick it out, you get grit points for doing so.

We still hold on to our belief that one must just soldier on through a difficult job because there is a pot of gold at the end of even the least-enjoyable rainbows: that social security check and tropical retirement home. At one of my husband's former workplaces, employees would end meetings by going around the table and saying their retirement date, which was sometimes years and years in the future. To me that seems like a bizarre way to go through life—just waiting for that time when you can actually have fun and enjoy being on the planet. But that's what the American dream has looked like for decades.

That dream is changing, of course, in large part because of

broader shifts going on in the workforce. Baby boomers had an expectation that they would stay with the same employer for forty years, gather a pension to pair with their monthly social security payout, and retire to a golf course in Arizona or Florida. That was the promise, and it was an excellent reason to persist and not quit, because the longer you stayed on, the greater your pension. Generation X had that promise for a small portion of its work life, but as companies dropped their pension plans and people started working for multiple employers over their working lives, that financial arrangement changed radically. Even the notion of retirement, and what it looks like, has changed. Now Gen Y and Millennials face not only a future devoid of employment-based pensions at all but also questions about whether even social security will be available for them. The corporate parent no longer looks out for the employee the way it once did, and therefore there is no longer any concept of loyalty to that corporate entity. So there are very few incentives to stick around for any length of time.

We're not at the point, yet, where quitting has become the norm, but it's possible that as Millennials age and raise their own children with a different idea of what quitting means, it could become easier to do so and more widely accepted by, say, employers who are looking at résumés featuring a lot of job-hopping.

Meanwhile, the rest of us have to be pioneers, and Jean Powell is one of them. She was in the beer business for years as the director of sales for a company that designed and made tap handles. "I find the smell of malt and the sight of stainless steel intoxicating," she wrote on her blog, *Jean on Tap.* Pun intended, I assume, and who wouldn't want that job? "It was my dream job," she told me. "But I really sacrificed myself because of the amount of physical time and attention it required to build this into a sales organization and build relationships across the industry. I'm grateful for it, but I will say it came at a cost to myself and my marriage." She knew it was time to move on to something else but struggled with the idea of leaving something she loved. "Why do you do that?" she asked herself. "Does that mean that you really don't love it? It showed a lot of parallels in my life with marriage and work that you can love something but maybe it's not meant for you."

Jean had quit other jobs before, but never without having a plan in place.

"I grew up thinking you kind of make your way through jobs and see how employers respond to résumés, that those long tenures mean something to them," she told me. "You have stability, you have loyalty. It means you know how to succeed. And as I went through this sort of transformation [in how I thought about my career], I decided I didn't necessarily equate the two. Because humans evolve and change. But even if you move up in an organization, most companies still have one dimension. They have one rallying cry, they have one vision, and that's not a bad thing. I can handle that structure, but I realized it's not for me."

But even with that realization, she had a tough time quitting. She wanted something decisive to happen at work so she would be able to pull the cord, something that would shove her out. "It's almost like you're in a relationship that's going downhill," she said, "and you're waiting for the other person to do that thing that makes you explode in an unreasonable fight so that you have a reason to walk out the door. Please do something to me that justifies this so that I know this was supposed to be. But if anything, only good things are happening right now! And here I am, kind of in the sea of saying 'Please do something to me so I'll be able to tell people that's why I left.'"

She would rather have been pushed than to quit of her own accord—that's how stigmatized quitting has become. I've heard some people say the same thing about skydiving—that it's easier if you tell someone to push you out of the plane than it is to just do it yourself. But ultimately, Jean told me, she stopped worrying about what that looked like to anyone else. "I realized that I had spent all this time climbing this ladder and I had gotten to the top and looked around and thought, 'Ah, this is a really great view, but this isn't the house I wanted to build.' I've achieved a lot of things, and I've gained a lot from the experience, and I'm incredibly positive about it all, but I don't necessarily think there's a lot left that I'm excited about except to start a new path. [In this job] I've been incredibly successful at building a lot of other people's dreams . . . but I think I've finally come to a point where I know somewhere in there is my own dream, and I want to honor that."

III

Courtenay Hameister's lament that if she quit her job she was quitting herself also reminds me of a common refrain I hear from people who say they can't just leap, because they have put so much time, energy, resources, time, blood, sweat, tears, and time into establishing a career. If you quit, won't all that feel as though it was a big waste of time? In finance, it's called the "sunk-cost fallacy." Investors resist dumping a bad stock because they've held on to it for so long and they've already sunk so much money into it. Peg Streep writes about this fallacy in the context of career changes, saying, "The investment of time and energy—and the unwillingness to quit and call it a lost cause—keeps people in place. People are far less inclined to take a risk in the name of gain, but they are willing to do almost anything to avoid a certain loss."

Yes, you may have put in a lot of years doing one thing and getting really good at that one thing. Lots of people asked me how I could leave radio journalism when I was so good at it and had devoted my entire career to it. Well, you know what? It was hard! But history shouldn't be the thing that keeps you from trying something new or from finding a better place to practice those mad skills you do have. The things you've learned and become expert at don't just go away—you always have them. Maybe you're figuring out new and different ways to utilize them, or maybe you find that you really *are* done with them and you are ready to move on to the next challenge. But whatever happens, all that time learning how to be good at something made you who you are and taught you how to learn—a skill that will serve you no matter what you're doing.

I love what Carl Seidman suggests to mitigate this notion. I mentioned in Chapter 2 that Carl had spent several years with a Big Four accounting firm before his leap. "Several people told me I should stick around for a few more years so that I could pocket more money in salary and bonuses," he said. "Some people questioned my sanity or whether I was a closet-but-well-functioning drug addict. Yet, the vast majority told me I was doing the right thing. Even the CEO, who ordered me to attend a one-on-one breakfast with him at a high-end restaurant, told me he would do what I'm doing if he could. The majority of people said that if they didn't feel locked in or the pressure of the firm, family, society, or financial expectations, they would do the same thing. Sadly, some of these people who had the same inclination to leave told me that they were just too scared to leave without certainty. How would future employers view the gap in their résumés? Would their skills be relevant to a different firm? Most people who hear my story don't comprehend the mechanics of actually going through with it and seeing it to fruition. I say there is really no such thing as absolute certainty—there are only hedges, and many of them are just psychological. You have to trust yourself that you are making the right decision. At the end of the day, very little is absolutely permanent."

Carl, by the way, has a wonderful take on quitting—he even gave a name to his first "quit." He called it his "first retirement": "It's not starting over!" he says. "That's what I tell a lot of people who talk to me about what I'm doing. They ask, 'Don't you feel like you're starting over again?' [And what I say is,] Take your résumé and put it in a drawer. Don't burn it. Just put it in a drawer. You know what? A year later open up the drawer, and it will still be there, and it won't have changed because you won't have changed. Your mind, your body, you may have experienced new things, but just because you took a year off or whatever it is, it doesn't mean you lose your college degree. It doesn't mean you lose the one year you spent doing this, the eight years you spent doing that. It's still part of who you are. It's still in your brain. It's still in every cell of your body. So what makes you think that just because you take a step back or you go in a different direction, you're going to lose it all?"

Carl blows away the sunk-cost fallacy. He's looking forward

to his second and third retirements and beyond, and he has an incredibly healthy perspective on what it means to quit and not know what's coming next, and not to worry that you're leaving behind the entirety of your experience and expertise. (Carl has so many great thoughts on the subject that I urge you to read more about it on his blog if you're interested [*The First Retirement*].) Societal conditioning is what makes us fear that our résumés and skills will go up in smoke if we step off of our career path. Society reacts to you as if you're losing everything you've built over time if you quit, and you can never get it back. This is absurd on its face, but in a culture in which you're always expected to be moving forward, people can't wrap their heads around the idea of putting their résumés in a drawer.

And this isn't just a career-related condition. I remember people saying something similar when I quit piano lessons my senior year in high school after twelve years of classical training. Twelve years up in smoke! All that time and energy (and cost to my parents!) wasted! Surely I would lose all those skills over the years. And yes, they got rusty. But I went back to it when I was thirty-five years old, and you know what? It took a lot of practice, but the knowledge was still there. It was hard work to get that part of my brain back in shape—especially the part that has to remember all of the notes above and below the staff—but it did come back. It's a muscle you have to retrain and exercise after years of no workouts. But the cliché about remembering how to ride a bike is a cliché because it's true. You do something long enough, and it becomes part of your DNA.

Quitting doesn't wipe out your history. Nothing can, really—skills you've mastered will always be there. If you get rusty, you can brush up. Reengaging with your dormant skills is a matter of having the self-discipline to make yourself practice. And if you come upon a potential employer who looks askance at the months or years you took off, and the company doesn't want to hire you because of it, then I'd argue you probably don't want to work there anyway. Why go through the risks of leaping only to return to a place that doesn't understand it? If enough of us preach this kind of employment compassion, maybe it will become a norm.

❙❙❙

There are approximately one million quotes about ambition, but I think of all people, Marcus Aurelius best captured our modern ethos: "A man's worth is no greater than his ambitions."

Thanks, pal.

Ambition is a cruel taskmaster. You can reap enormous rewards from it, but once you hop on the ambition train, the idea of jumping off it feels like all kinds of self-sabotage. And I think that keeps a lot of aspirational people—people who define success by a constant upward trajectory—from leaping from their jobs.

I never put much thought into why it was so important to me to have a cool job, or a publicly cool job at that. I'd always said, from the time I was in high school, that it was more important to me to be somehow famous than it was to be rich. (Given those parameters, public radio was the perfect place to land.) I don't come from a famous family. I don't come from a big city where I would have been influenced by fame or fortune. But I know myself well enough to know that a lot of my striving, even from childhood, had to do with that hunger for ... attention, I guess? External approval? Some combination of neuroses that made the prospect of quitting almost painful.

The source of my ambition is another one of the subjects I quizzed my parents on after I made the leap. I wanted to know if they had some sense of where it came from.

"I think all the things in our lives add up to who we are," my mom answered. "So all the things, whether they were successes or, in your mind, failures have built your internal drive. And that's the composite of all those pieces. And somehow, deep inside, you have that drive. Why you have that and somebody else doesn't, I don't know."

My dad had a different take.

"I think one of the biggest drivers of ambition is lack of self-confidence and lack of comfort in your own skin," he said. "And I think you were really unhappy with yourself. And, therefore, you were driven to succeed. Because that makes you feel better."

Truth bomb: dropped. I knew he was right. I hated to admit that my own psychological weakness was what propelled me to, in essence, prove myself to the world by attaining some notion of mass recognition. But it did. And maybe that's why quitting felt so scary, because in some twisted way, it made me feel as if I had been foolish to try to fly so high.

"A lot of people are like that," Dad assured me. "It's a sensation I've never felt because I've always been comfortable with myself." (Dad! Why didn't you give me *those* genes?) "Therefore, I really have not been driven. I'm not competitive. That, in some ways, is a disadvantage. But somebody can sit you down and say you've got all this talent, and it won't mean a darn thing to you because you don't believe it. And that lack of belief in yourself is something that I think people have a horrendous time solving. And maybe never solve it."

Hearing my dad talk about my insecurity being the driving force for my ambition suddenly made so much sense. It helped me understand what was so scary about quitting *Marketplace* that I hadn't anticipated before I left. I'd always held up my job as the most impressive thing about myself, and I now no longer had anything I could show to prove to people that I was awesome. I no longer had cool attached to my name. As I said in my WDS speech, I was no longer "*Marketplace*'s Tess Vigeland." I was just Tess Vigeland. And I'd never really believed that she was remarkable and special outside of what she did for a living.

The social scholar Brene Brown has written extensively about this, and her book *Daring Greatly* provided a lot of comfort for me in the months following my leap. She talks a lot about shame, and her research suggesting that shame is a significant factor in keeping successful people from leaping rang true with me.

"You've designed a product or written an article or created a piece of art that you want to share with a group of friends," Brown writes in the book. "Sharing something that you've created is a vulnerable but essential part of engaged and wholehearted living. It's the epitome of daring greatly. But because of how you were raised or how you approach the world, you've knowingly or unknowingly attached your self-worth to how your product or art is received. In simple terms, if they love it, you're worthy; if they don't, you're worthless."

I think that need for approval can be extended beyond just an article or a piece of art to an entire career, an entire body of work such that, if you get positive responses to it on a regular basis, those responses feed your ambition, and it is very hard to imagine living without them. And what I feared in many ways was that in leaping I would not just be quitting, but, ultimately, I would also be letting the ambition seep out of me like a leaky balloon.

Carl Seidman has a theory about this aspect of the leap—he calls it his "theory of conditioning," and basically it says that for most people, ambition is based on their surroundings. "I went to a nationally ranked public high school, and the only measurement that was used to determine that was how many kids took advanced placement exams. So I felt like an idiot if I wasn't taking as many advanced placement exams as everybody else. Many people went to this Ivy League school and that medical school, and if you didn't go, you felt like a failure. Whereas if you grew up down the street across the city limits and attended the school where the kids didn't take advanced placement exams, if you didn't take them, that wouldn't be that big a deal. So I think being part of an upbringing or a society or a culture where there is this expectation to perform and this expectation to be exceptional, if you're not, you feel like an idiot. If there isn't that expectation and you succeed, all of a sudden at that downtrodden school you're the king of the world just by comparison."

Now obviously, plenty of ambitious people come out of difficult situations, and Carl's not saying that's at all unusual. But there is a pressure that comes from expectations that are set early by your surroundings. And no matter where those expectations come from, they can be hard to live up to time after time after time.

Carl attended the World Domination Summit (WDS),

where I gave my speech, and he said the whole idea of being "remarkable in a conventional world," while an admirable goal, also placed a significant premium on grand ambition. I'm sure that's the case with a lot of conferences like WDS, where attendees are looking for ways to better themselves and the world around them. But Carl noted the pressure that accompanies any cheerleading around entrepreneurial endeavors.

"I met a lot of people there," he said, "who felt really bad about themselves, who said, 'You know, I hear all these really interesting people doing all sorts of cool stuff, and I'm not, and should I feel bad about that? What if I just want to go into a nine-to-five job and just do what's expected of me and not have to think that hard and not have to prove myself, and then come home and spend Friday night with my boyfriend or girlfriend, and that's my life. Why is that not OK?' And I don't know what the answer to that is. It's easy for me to say, 'You don't have to compete. You don't have to prove yourself. You don't have to get out there and show what's so great about you.' But I fear that in our society, the media all around us—Facebook, Instagram, *American Idol*, and so many others—are saying, 'You know what? The average Joe and the average Jane, you can all be exceptional, and you have to want to be that, and you have to take the steps to get that celebrity, to get noticed, to be something different!' But I don't think you do."

I agree—I don't think you do either. For some potential leapers, good enough just isn't good enough, and the idea that you would voluntarily give up and give in, in relation to your career, is almost too much to even contemplate. I get it, believe me; that's how I've lived a good portion of my life. And I think that's why I put so much pressure on myself to find something new right away, because otherwise I was letting this part of me go that was the only thing that was bringing me external validation: my ambition was driving my success. Leave the ambition; lose the success. That's not true, of course, but it's hard to recognize that letting go of ambition in one area of your life doesn't mean you're giving up anything. It just means your priorities might change. And that can be a great thing.

I can't tell you how to get over that hurdle—you'll have to figure that out for yourself. For me, as I've just noted, I had to tell myself that this was going to be an incredibly short break and that I'd transition into something new very quickly, almost as if it had never happened and that life would go on as it was supposed to. The further away I got from "short break," however, the more I worried, until I realized that ambition doesn't have to be pointed in a single direction. I found new interests, and I'm still waiting to see what might come along that catches my eye.

I haven't lost my ambition. I'm just charging its batteries for a while.

III

The first thing that happens when you figure out what you want to do with your life is you write down how you're going to do it. Right? You make a plan. You go through the steps that will get you to your ultimate goal. And then you set out on whatever path that is, checking off milestones along the way. From the moment of that first list, you have, and are expected to have, the one-year plan, the two-year plan, and the five- and ten-year plans.

When you leap, or think you might want to, there is no plan, at least not one that you can point to and say, "Oh! Here's what I do next!" And what that means is that your future is one giant blob of uncertainty. And for most of us, That. Is. Terrifying.

Fear of the unknown is what keeps so many people in jobs they no longer love. Most of us don't jump out of planes, because the idea seems so crazy and risky, and most of us, for the same reasons, don't leave careers or jobs without a plan. But here's the thing to remember: the safety we build around ourselves is, by and large, an illusion. That's why I love—and now try to live by—that quote, attributed to Voltaire, about uncertainty being an uncomfortable position, but certainty being an absurd one. It's true. Anything can happen at any time. What matters is how we respond to it and how we prepare for it.

Wendy Harris, the former attorney, believes that the fear of uncertainty really boils down to the fear of failure. If you don't have a plan—don't even know what your plan is—then there's a bigger chance that things will end up going badly. And that's what kept her from leaping sooner than she did. "What I kept saying to myself was, this could totally not work. And just trying to find a way to be comfortable with that was the challenge. You kind of have to be willing to have it be a colossal failure and say, Wow, that's really something, but isn't it cool that I tried. And you know, I was sitting in my office in New York on September 11, 2001. I know that for me, I started looking at mortality in a way that I never had before. This idea that you just don't know what life's going to bring. Why not enjoy life now?"

Wendy no longer has five- or ten-year plans. She says the most she'll pencil in is six months. "I've learned that if you overplan too much, you're either disappointed, or it just never goes how you expected. And yes, it's terrifying in a way. That's why more people don't do this. It's why I kept moving the date of when I was going to leave."

For me the discomfort wasn't just not having a long-term plan but that I didn't even really have a short-term one. The uncertainty was immediate—I worried about what those first few months would be like and how I'd deal with the fact that my life had taken such a radical turn. I had no idea what would sustain me if I didn't have a news cycle, a microphone, or a story to write.

For Nat Katz, what he didn't realize was how much he'd miss his community, which was the student population at Harvard University. Earlier in my career, Nat and I worked in the same office, for the same company (the parent company of *Marketplace*), but I barely knew who he was, except that he was six feet, six inches tall and therefore somewhat hard to miss. Several years later, after we'd both left that company, I found a note from him in my message box on Facebook. He'd just departed his job as the Epps Fellow, a chaplain position, at Harvard's Memorial Church—where he'd been a primary provider of spiritual guidance for students on campus.

Nat had left California several years earlier, after deciding to pursue a career that fit with what was already a huge part of his life—the church. He had been accepted by Harvard Divinity School, and upon graduating, he was planning to move back west. But instead, he was invited by one of Harvard's great theologians, the Rev. Professor Peter Gomes, to stay at the school and become the Epps Fellow. It was, in his line of work, a Big-Time Job. He worked with Gomes (who also authored the book *The Good Life*, which I recommend to anyone contemplating their life's work), until Gomes's death in 2011, after which he helped keep the ministry in good hands while the university searched for a new church leader. He stayed in that job for a couple of years, working at Memorial Church, until for various reasons, some relating to office politics, Nat concluded that it was time to leave Harvard. He figured he could return to LA to complete his ordination process, thinking that he could work out the whole job thing once he got there. But for all the spiritual wisdom he had gained over both his career and lifetime, none of it truly prepared him for what it would be like to leave his job and not know what would come next.

"Initially, I was planning to leave the day after helping with the commencement services for the undergrads. But then I decided that was insane and instead I gave myself, I think it was five days, and I shipped out all my stuff and tried to tie up as many loose ends as I could. At a certain point, I was just looking forward to having space, knowing that there was a lot that I needed to process. I got to LA, and for about the first month, I was not worried about it. I was just going to enjoy myself. And then it started to catch up with me that I didn't know who I was now. I wasn't at the church. I wasn't going to be going back to the church. There had to be things that I needed to be doing and places that I needed to be and people who needed me to be in those places. I also started to miss the students. And I had this negative, essential question: What's my meaning? What am I here for?"

I asked how he got through that moment, or moments, and he said something so profoundly practical that I remember laughing:

"There was this period when I was just annoyed and frustrated. All of my relationships felt very stressed because suddenly I was putting so much expectation on those people. I didn't have these other things where I would normally be getting my sense of value and purpose and meaning."

I hadn't really thought of it before, but that seemed logical. You go from having a purpose—in Nat's case, a truly higher purpose!—for a good chunk of the day (or in the case of a chaplain or a newsperson, twenty-four hours a day, seven days a week) to having nothing to do, or certainly nothing as consequential as what you did at your place of work. It happens rather suddenly, even if you've had time to prepare for it, and filling that void can take some doing.

And when you're leaving one of the biggest brand names in the world—Harvard!—the void can seem cosmic:

"Coming out of being at Harvard, the unspoken assumption is, well, if you're leaving, it must be for something really extraordinary. I had a narrative that was factually very true, which was, 'I don't necessarily have anything lined up, but I'm really focused on my ordination process, and there's a lot to get ready for that ... ,' so I did not have to cope with verbalizing over and over that I didn't know what I was going to do. You're saying it as much to convince yourself as to convince anybody else."

But the roller coaster does have its upsides, as we've already noted, and for Nat, that time of unease led to something new:

"You go through this period of having all this prestige,

or fill in the blank, in the environment that you came from. Then you start to shed that, right? I was being forced to let go of stuff, the baggage I didn't know I was carrying. Then suddenly, you turn around, and at first, you're in that mode of feeling like, 'Something is really different. That's really uncomfortable.' Then after a period of time, 'I feel lighter because I'm not carrying stuff.'" And by "stuff," he was talking about everything from the pressure of an upward trajectory in your career to the concerns about what other people think of you when you leap. "Then I started seeing ways of being myself that I hadn't been able to see before because I'd been too caught up in all the things I was responsible for. I had to fulfill duty and responsibility first, before I could think about taking care of things for myself."

Nat didn't spend more than a couple of months wandering in the wilderness before he found a perfect fit for what he realized he wanted to do next. And he was ordained as an Episcopal priest a year and a half after his leap. But, clearly, stewing in the uncertainty brought him a clarity he lacked concerning both his purpose and where he wanted to devote his time and talents.

III

I would predict that any potential leaper will face at least one of these psychological hurdles, if not all three. And that makes total sense. But one piece of advice that Peg Streep gave me has stuck with me: the more often you quit, the better you get at quitting. And, in reality, we quit things all the time—maybe not always our jobs, but we quit volunteer posts, we quit toxic relationships, we quit chores, we quit things that are good for us, such as . . . running! Each time we quit, we become better at dealing with uncertainty and more comfortable with the idea of change within ourselves. And then when change is forced on us, we're better equipped to handle it.

6.
LEANING OUT
AND
CLIMBING
DOWN

I mentioned earlier that my ambition made it tough for me to appreciate just how far I'd gotten in my career when I got the host job at *Marketplace Money*. It was a huge gig, high profile, and it put me in rarified air near the top of my industry. But I wanted more. I felt as if I was still part of a second tier, in terms of audience size and recognition of the show within our industry. I wanted to be in the first tier of public radio talent. It's not that I didn't appreciate what I did have, but it just wasn't enough.

Sheryl Sandberg, Facebook COO and bestselling author of *Lean In*, would be proud of that. I leaned in, as much as I knew how. I wanted more, and I asked for more—repeatedly. I was never any good at negotiating for more pay or a better title, but that never stopped me from trying. (For example, I always wanted the "host and senior editor" title that was afforded to the host of the afternoon *Marketplace* program, but each time I asked about it, there was some excuse not to give it to me. To my eternal discredit, I backed down.) But no matter where

I was on the ladder, I was always seeking and pining for a higher rung. That's what we're all supposed to do, right? Especially in promoting and furthering the cause of women in the workplace.

For many of us, ambition is something that we are conditioned to feel from childhood and throughout our working lives. We assume and believe that every step on the career ladder must and will be an upward trajectory. You go to college. Then you get a job. Then you get a better job. And then a better job after that. And that goes on and on until you are president of the United States. Or an astronaut. Or Kim Kardashian. OK, maybe not that last one. But even if you'll never have *those* fancy titles, you're often taught to always be striving for something bigger, better, and more impressive than the last thing you did.

In some ways, of course, that is the natural order of things. You get better and more experienced, you get promoted, you move up in your job or your industry, and titles and money go with those steps up the ladder. If you're ambitious, you're not content with lateral moves or stasis, and you certainly don't contemplate stepping down a rung or two, or—heaven forbid—stepping off the ladder altogether. It's just not done.

So when I left, I worried about whether taking my dice and going somewhere else would be seen as a step down, as giving up on the career I had built over twenty years. And I wasn't just worried about what everybody else thought. I worried about what a step down might do to my own sense of self. Was I giving up my ambition? Had I lost it? It's a real question that you have to confront if you're facing a void of not knowing what to do next in your career.

I had a great discussion once with my friend J. D. Roth

about these great expectations that we place on ourselves and that we assume others have placed on us. J.D. and I met when I interviewed him in 2011 at a financial bloggers conference that I covered for *Marketplace*. He's the founder of the website getrichslowly.org. We became friends, and he's the one who invited me to speak at World Domination Summit in 2013. As we talked about expectations, we ruminated on what would happen if we just gave the middle finger to the success ladder and became baristas at Starbucks. (You may remember I also joked about this with my father.) It's a perfectly respectable job, with decent pay and good benefits. I'm sure it's more difficult than most of us imagine from the other side of the counter—I would probably punch out a customer who took five minutes to explain exactly how she wanted a single coffee drink to be made. But essentially, you make coffee for people all day, and then you do it again the next day. Nobody expects any more from you than just doing that and doing it well. (I'm sure there are plenty of opportunities for ambition at every company, including Starbucks. And much respect to my Pasadena baristas who make an Iced-Venti-Red-Eye-Two-Pumps-Classic to *perfection*.)

But what we were really asking ourselves was this: What would it mean to get off the hamster wheel that says that each phase of your career has to be at least as awesome, if not more so, than the last thing you did? What if you didn't have to live up to anyone's expectations, including your own, to be bigger and better with every passing year? You make coffee, you go home.

The problem arises when you know you can do more than what you're currently doing, whether it's because of your skill set or your colleagues or your dreams, or some combination thereof. And you feel like you *should* do more because of all the opportunities you've had and the deep experience you've gained from those opportunities. What you worry about is failing to live up to what you've already accomplished and your expectations for yourself. It is a giant boulder that will sit on your shoulders if you leap.

No matter what your next steps are—up the ladder, down the ladder, or off the ladder entirely—the process of figuring out how to remove that weight of expectation, or at least lessen the load, is an invaluable one. You can learn a lot from just giving yourself a freaking break.

III

Personal reinvention is the buzz-concept of our time. The rise of technology has made it possible for all of us—we're told—to pursue our passions and become whomever and whatever we want, at almost any point in our lives. There have never been more resources, more avenues, or more cheerleading for becoming something new. Some*one* new. Naturally, if you're going to take a leap from your career, it's because you are going to reinvent! Yay for you!

But whom do we celebrate when it comes to reinvention? The people who went on to even greater success and bigger careers. Vera Wang started as a fashion editor for *Vogue*, then became a world-famous designer of wedding gowns and other frocks well into her career. George Foreman is known at least as much for his grills as he is for his boxing career and the Rumble in the Jungle. Martha Stewart was a model and a stockbroker before becoming the Martha Stewart we know today. We very rarely celebrate people who step off the fast track and reinvent themselves into something less traditionally ambitious. And I suppose in a lot of ways that makes sense, because we rightly value high-profile accomplishment; we like to applaud people who've made it to the top. Maybe we don't applaud those who decide to step down or off the ladder of success because we just don't hear about it. It's a quieter reinvention. But I wonder if we also assume they lack ambition and therefore aren't worthy of celebration.

When you set out to reinvent, when you leap without knowing what's next, you will feel pressure to continue on some undefined yet upward trajectory. In those first few months after leaving *Marketplace*, my mind was spinning through the possibilities of every conceivable new career. I pondered getting a certification to become a Master Gardener—I love sinking my hands into dirt, planting a seed, watching what happens over the next weeks, months, and years, and then sitting back and enjoying the fruits of that effort . . . sometimes literally. I've always been interested in crisis management and preparation—not corporate, but things like natural disasters and tragedies—so I thought maybe I could be boots-on-the-ground for a relief organization. I even tossed around the idea of whether I could start a catering company—I love cooking and throwing parties, so why not combine the two? So many ideas swirled around my head. People told me to buy this book or that book to find out how to pursue this passion or that one (I never did find out what color my parachute was) or to even figure out how to be a gardener-caterer in a disaster zone. I'd certainly be carving my own path on that one.

All of these things appealed to me except for one small

issue: they felt like a far step away from what I'd been doing, and I didn't want to start at the bottom of a new ladder. And yes, perhaps that's the point, and maybe it would be exciting and fresh and I could sink my hands or my teeth or whatever into an entirely new career. But that meant giving up a twenty-year ambition to be at the very top of the ladder I'd already climbed. At least I thought that's what it meant.

❚❚❚

The problem was that I was confusing my job with my talents.

My friend Adam Ragusea once said to me, "People don't love you for personal finance. People love you 'cause you're the lady who lives in the radio."

We were chatting on the phone, almost a year after I had left *Marketplace*, about my possibly doing a podcast. "It's your jam!" he said. I told him that I had no idea what people wanted to hear from me anymore. It was a version of something I'd said in the WDS speech, where I worried about whether I'd lose Facebook friends and Twitter followers because I was no longer a fancy national broadcaster. I know those things aren't supposed to be important, but, to me, they were an external validation of my importance on earth. The idea of a podcast flummoxed me, because I figured most of the people in any potential audience would expect me to talk about personal finance, or business and economics, the things they identified me with on the air. Why would they listen to me talk about anything other than that? It was a problem because it was the one subject I absolutely didn't want to talk about anymore.

I loved Adam's immediate response about my relationship with my being a voice in people's ears—"It's your jam!"—but then I wondered again what I was losing by leaving the air-waves. Sure, I could start a podcast, and I could figure out some subject that I enjoyed, and *maybe* people would follow me to it. But I was still hanging on to that notion of being a radio personality, and I was convinced that without that kind of ca-chet and institutional branding, I would never attract enough attention and listenership to make the effort worthwhile. So I dropped the idea. I dropped the idea because I was afraid of failure, and I dropped the idea because I was sure that what really attracted people to me was that I was on a national radio show. That was what made me worthy of their time and atten-tion. My identity was so tied up in being the lady who lived in the radio—personal finance or otherwise—that I couldn't see how I was valuable to others outside of that existence. And in turn I resisted looking into opportunities that wouldn't push me further up a mythical ladder that, if I'm being honest with myself, no one else cared about.

And while I'm being honest, I'll also admit that I was prob-ably being lazy. I'd spent the last ten years with a staff that did a lot of the grunt work for me. I had bookers to line up interviews, production assistants to help log tape (listen to the audio from an interview and transcribe it), and producers and directors to herd all the cats into place before we went on the air. That made it, psychologically, really difficult to absorb the idea of doing my own podcast without any help. It's not rocket science—not by a long shot—but I was just so used to having super-qualified people around me doing a lot of heavy lifting that I winced at the idea of having to do it all myself. I'm afraid that may qualify me as a diva, which, if true, would be my worst nightmare.

But this is the way of the office, isn't it? The higher up you go, the less responsible you have to be for scut work. Even if you'd be really good at that scut work because you had perfected it earlier in your career. In other words, I had all the skills to put together a podcast, no problem. What I didn't have was a rope to strangle that voice inside my head that kept saying, "If you do this, you're going back down the ladder!" I think this is also why I didn't pursue jobs at other public radio stations. I'd had my own *national* show, for Pete's sake. Going to a local station? For anything less than a top-host job (which are few and far between)? That meant I was moving waaaay down the corporate ladder to a position that I had exceeded years earlier. Instead of leaning in, it was definitely leaning out.

I fought this mental battle constantly. I was holding out for that next perfect dream job that was probably never going to come along, and I was doing that because I was a big baby who wouldn't just go do a job that anybody else would have thought was totally cool. It was radio show host—preferably national—or bust. That was probably stupid and arrogant and foolish on my part, and I certainly couldn't blame anyone else for my not getting another job in public radio by then. But I also worried that if I took a "lesser" role (and I use quotation marks because, really, "lesser" is extremely relative here), I could have been unhappy if it felt like a step down.

III

Christy Moe Marek loves her work at a bakery in Minnesota. She's been there for twelve years, starting as a baker and now serving as both a baker and general manager. But before becoming an expert in all thing yeast, she spent ten years in corporate America, until she was laid off from her job as a technical writer and software trainer at a bank.

The bakery gig came after several months of trying to start her own business and, in her words, failing miserably and having no idea what to do next. "I knew I wanted something physical," she said, "and there was an opening for a baker at the Great Harvest Bread Company, which had opened just down the street from us. Even though I didn't have any experience with baking other than in my own home, I applied for the job, and the owner and I completely hit it off. Whereas I would go into some corporate interview and they'd see that I had moved around from job to job and give me a hard time for it, the owner at Great Harvest looked at my résumé and said, 'Wow, you've done a lot of really cool things,' and I thought, This is where I belong!" It was a 50 percent pay cut from her previous job, but she thought, This is where I need to be.

Despite her love of that new career, a little voice in her head kept saying, "You should be doing something bigger and better." It got louder and louder and harder to tune out.

"The issue I've always had is that I'm working beneath my potential. Completely overqualified for what I'm doing there," she said. "There's a part of me that feels I should be doing more in my job, or at least I should have published a book or done something else 'spectacular' with this lifestyle that the bakery affords me. Maybe letting go of this need to do more, to be a success from a societal perspective, is a part of it. Am I happy? Most days I am. Then why the nagging feeling that I need to be accomplished somehow?"

That nagging feeling is a cruel taskmaster. If you can ask

yourself, "Am I happy?" and have the answer on most days be "Yes, I am," you shouldn't have second thoughts, right? How is happiness every day not enough for any of us? And who's to say Christy is working beneath her potential? She's a baker! A skill I—and many others—would divinely love to have. She makes people happy every day when they come into the bakery and buy the things she has made.

But I totally get what she's saying. She went from a traditional job at a bank to a more, shall we say, artisanal career, which no doubt fed her anxiety about how she defined her own success. "The idea of a career track seems outdated," she said. "My drive to end up in the corporate world because I thought that's where I was supposed to be if I was going to 'make it' . . . maybe I'm a little Mary Tyler Mooreish! But that really strikes me as being sort of a fallacy. I mean it's great to have dreams, great to have goals, great to have things that you want to do with your life. But feeling that somehow our worth is tied to these things? I think it would take a significant change in how society works and how our culture works on the little minds of us all. It would take a lot."

Yes. Yes, it would. Because for all the Happy Talk about how we should define success by personal satisfaction, and maybe by our giving something back to the community, what we really want to know is what your paycheck looks like. Or how much your house cost. Remember that? That water cooler conversation from the early 2000s where everybody talked about what they paid for their house and how much it had gone up in value in the last two seconds?

In a celebrity culture, a rabid consumer culture, we all know what success is supposed to look like. Not only are you happy but you also have a fancy title, you have money, you're probably on TV at least once in a while, and people know Who You Are. You've accomplished something significant (even if "significant" is blockbuster ratings as a cast member of *Jersey Shore*), and you've been rewarded for it. That is success as we know it in America. It's about how much money we have, how many things we can buy, even how many Twitter followers and Facebook "likes" we've amassed, rather than how much of a difference we've made in people's lives, or how much we've improved the planet.

Christy started a blog several years ago called *Wonder of All Things* as a place for her to put thoughts to virtual paper and share them with whoever might visit. But she admitted it serves a second purpose: as proof that she does more than proof dough. "I could justify that I was not just a baker or a general manager, whatever, by saying, 'Oh, but I have this blog, and I wrote a memoir that's sitting in a drawer, and I have all these other things that I've done.' It does feel like there always has to be something else, because what I'm doing on its own as a career somehow can't be enough."

She still struggles with the idea that somehow she's not living up to her potential—at least the potential as defined by that amorphous collective we call "society." So I asked her how she deals with the self-doubt and how *she* fights against those constant cultural expectations to lean in and climb up. "Last Christmas," she answered, "was the first time at the bakery I really considered the impact that we had on the customers and on their holidays and their get-togethers and that sort of thing. And then I shifted my perspective a bit and really allowed myself to take in, you know, 'Yeah, it might just be a loaf of bread, but this is somebody's tradition. And this is somebody's family gathering.' Sometimes all it takes for us to find the meaning in what we're doing is just to have that shift in our perspective and get out of the whole big cultural societal framework of what success is and what we should be striving for. There is so much more depth and meaning in our lives if we're able to do that. But we need to define that for ourselves and to find peace in it from there."

III

Christy is an example of a leaper who went into something entirely different from what she used to do. She learned a whole set of new skills. She climbed all the way down the ladder and started over on the bottom rung of a completely different ladder. But sometimes as you're climbing down, you find there's another way up the ladder, using the skills you already have. That's what happened after Karen Kiefaber leaped . . . after she retired, actually, at age forty-six.

Karen spent almost her entire career in retail, despite a lifelong yearning to be a star of stage and screen. Before entering retail, she had attended the American Academy of Dramatic Arts in New York, but, she said, "I saw all these actors struggling and getting turned away, and I wanted to make money!" So instead of going into acting, in her early twenties she got a part-time job with the upscale department store Nordstrom, and she ended up as a buyer for eight years. She loved being paid to think about what merchandise sells and what merchandise doesn't sell and why, as well as whether mallard blue or sky blue would be the "in" color for a given season. She became well known in retail for her knack for spotting trendy accessories. And that talent is what caught the eye of the founder of Hot Topic, the shopping mall mainstay that specializes in music-related and goth fashion.

Karen became a key player in Hot Topic's explosion from a small private retailer with ten stores to a publicly traded company with outlets in almost every mall in America and beyond. When the company went public, she owned a boatload of options that, after several stock splits, made her a multimillionaire at age forty.

But far more than the money, Karen loved the job because of the access that came with the store's rock 'n' roll pop culture status. "I had backstage passes for everything. I would walk in, and everyone knew me at the House of Blues. I would go to the Skywalker Ranch and stay the weekend to preview the latest *Star Wars* film. I had become this kind of big shot, and it came very easily." It was her dream punk-rock job . . . at least until the company started to get too big, too unwieldy, and, for Karen, not as much fun. She was attending more and more meetings instead of going out and checking the pulse of teen America. She was no longer happy, and she felt as if she had plenty of financial freedom to just up and leave without knowing what might come next. So she did. In fact, she retired.

It was more difficult emotionally than she expected it to be. She was attached to the company, to the perks, and she wondered if she would no longer feel important once she stepped off that metal-studded, goth-punk ladder. "I kind of had this rock-star status, and I ended it myself. And, of course, I have questions about that—I don't regret it, but there was an adjustment. I think I tend to want to tell strangers what I used to do, to say that I used to be somebody. I feel embarrassed about that now—I should be able to get by on my own whatever. But all of a sudden, the thought that you don't look successful . . . it hurts the ego. It really does. People would say, 'Oh, she was so good at what she did. What does she do now? I think she volunteers at an animal shelter. Dude, what is up with that?'"

After some time to reflect and decompress from her Hot Topic career (lots and lots of walking around Pasadena's Rose Bowl), Karen threw herself into countless hours of relatively anonymous, unpaid, and largely thankless volunteer work at, yes, the Pasadena Humane Society and SPCA. She has helped raise hundreds of thousands of dollars, and she was invited to serve as board chair, among many other tasks.

But one question has stuck with her that a close friend asked upon her departure from Hot Topic: Don't you feel like you won't have a purpose? "And I've got to say, I've always had a purpose," Karen told me. "If I'm a window washer, I'm going to be the very best window washer. I'm not going to just brush dogs. I'm going to take over. I had a lot of business and marketing, so I felt like I was going to continue to have a purpose. What I didn't continue to have was rock-star status."

Now, Karen calls herself "the busiest person you know without a paycheck." Her definition of success is a far cry from what it was in the heady days of national retail. "Love. Happiness. My home. A great relationship with my family. A core group of dear friends, wonderful animals. I think that's all success." Maybe that's all easy to say because she had a nice nest egg to fall back on and she has already proven herself in the working world. But she was also able to successfully put her skills to a completely new and unexpected use, stepping perhaps across to a new ladder. "I still don't know what I want to be when I grow up," she says. "I think there's something else, and I don't know what it is. I really don't. But there's going to be something."

III

Plenty of people step off the ladder. Plenty of people go back down a few rungs. For me, the pressures are greatest when I think about starting over at the bottom of something. I think this is common, especially if you've been gathering experience in one career for a long time. Maybe you're not a diva (and please, please, please, let me not be one either!), but you are likely used to a certain amount of deference, a certain amount of access, a certain amount of assistance. Once you leap, you'll be without those things. Not everybody makes that adjustment easily, and it's natural for that change to feel a little shocking at first. In contemplating what comes next, you will find yourself asking how much of that you can live without.

But you know what you'll remember, eventually? You have skills, and those skills are, in all likelihood, transferable. Your job is separate from your skill set. You probably won't start over on the bottom rung—unless, of course, you want to.

III

A little while after my WDS talk in Portland, I was invited to host a daylong event at Chicago Ideas Week. The organizer asked if I would deliver a keynote and then emcee the rest of the day for something called the Edison Talks. I'd open the session, then introduce all of the other speakers throughout the day and conduct interviews with two of them on stage (movie director M. Night Shyamalan and *Boardwalk Empire* actor Michael Shannon).

I've always been comfortable with public speaking. Maybe it's because I did theater in high school, or maybe it was all those piano recitals. I've never shied away from microphones, and I love an audience. I'd given speeches throughout my career, usually to small groups of public radio donors, but sometimes to crowds of hundreds, especially while I was at *Marketplace,* where we received lots of requests for appearances to talk about the economy. Speaking from a stage to a large gathering of strangers is just not an issue for me the way it is for so many people—in fact, I thrive on it. So much so that I never thought of it as a skill. It was just something I did, both on the radio and off.

The event at Chicago Ideas Week came almost a year after I had left my job, and what the organizers asked me to do was not something I'd ever really even thought of as a potential career. Professional emcee, interviewer, and panel moderator? Huh. Turned out—I loved it. Interviews are my favorite thing. The stage is my favorite place. The microphone is my favorite accessory. How did I not think of this? Probably because I was stuck on the idea of an audience of millions and a staff of producers and a regular salaried position. This new opportunity had none of those. But it was something I was good at, something I enjoyed, and I had the skills that made it a great match, skills that most people don't have. Oh—and it paid too.

Maybe if I hadn't been so stubborn and resistant to traditional (to my mind, "cliché") methods of job searching, I would've discovered this kind of thing on my own. My guess is that I could have opened any career book or gone to any outplacement office, and they probably would have had me make a list of all the skills I used in my job. And I probably would have limited that list to technical things like these: I know digital editing, computer-based reporting, and the news, and I understand how to position a microphone. But you have to think beyond the talents that you've developed because of your career path. The things you just do so well that they're like a second skin are actually your greatest assets. The things you joke that you could "do in your sleep"? Those are skills, and you probably have some that make you very valuable, that other people do not have, and that you don't even think about when you list your qualifications. Start taking notice of those things. You might surprise yourself.

There are days when I still catch myself asking: Is this a step down from hosting my own national radio show with millions of listeners? But I'm slowly changing my own definition of what success means. I'm definitely changing my expectation of what it means to be ambitious. All of these issues were, and still are, tremendous hurdles to overcome. I don't think I'm comfortable yet with the idea of, say, making coffee for a living—but why not go to work for the Red Cross in disaster relief? Why not pursue photography? Why not lift that mantle of pressure to continue on some preordained upward trajectory? Diversify the dream.

I had a fantastic job, no doubt about it. I had a job people admired and looked up to. I had fans. How do you top that?

Here's a better question: Why do I expect that of myself? Why should anyone?

It's all tied up in letting go of an identity that is wrapped up in your career. And that is really, really hard. But part of the leaping process is letting go of the expectations you set for yourself and that you think others have set for you. It's a long process to shed that—for me, two years and counting. If you don't feel that pressure, congratulations! I wish I had the confidence to tell Societal Expectation to go to hell. You should shout it from the top of the ladder. Or whatever rung you're on. Or maybe we could just stop talking about success ladders altogether and focus on climbing in whatever direction will most fulfill us.

7.
THE
GRIND

So far I've covered a lot of the touchy-feely stuff that comes with taking a leap, but there's obviously much more to it than just figuring out what's going to make you feel worthy and valuable. Entire books have been written about the adjustments you have to make when you go from working in an office to working at home. And chances are, you will have at least a short period of time after your leap when *you* will be making those adjustments. You'll become what's often referred to as a "solo-preneuer"—someone who works at home, alone, running a business all by themselves. An entrepreneur starts out that way, but the goal is to fairly quickly have other people working for you. The rest of us stay solo. We're freelancers, contractors, consultants, advisers, and beyond, and we're completely independent. I'm pretty sure I've read every single one of those books about adjusting to self-employment, and I'll try to distill some of the wisdom here in some quick-and-dirty observations about what the daily grind means during a career transition. Bear in mind, these are my observations, and your experience could be different. But these are a few elements of the transition to working from home that I took note of, as well as some contributions from the sampling of people I've spoken with.

Expenses

The things you buy and use around the house will probably change, and it's going to be an expensive part of the transition. I buy far more paper than I used to because I don't have a "work printer" (and, yes, we should all use less paper, of course, but sometimes you just have to print stuff). You may have been that organized person who brought lunch to work, but you'll be making it all the time now because you're less likely to leave home, and you will probably be trying to save money. If you're like me, you'll learn how to turn just about every version of last night's dinner into a sandwich.

Where you'll save is at the gas pump. I used to commute twenty miles a day—which is *nothing* for LA—but now I fill up maybe once a month, depending on how much I need to travel for various freelance gigs. I also buy about a third of the new clothes I used to, and even that is probably a lot more than I actually need.

Taxes, Part 1

Get an accountant or tax attorney to do your taxes. I had always done ours with TurboTax, but being self-employed is just about the messiest thing you can do to your tax status, so I recommend that you get a professional. Consult with someone before you even start working for yourself so you know what receipts to save and what deductions you can take advantage of. Accountants can also advise you on setting up your own retirement plan and other savings vehicles and on dealing with health care costs.

If you have no fear, then by all means do your taxes yourself, but I'm decent with numbers and budgets, and I covered personal finance for six years, and I *still* would not dare tackle this on my own.

In and Out

Stay on top of your payables and receivables!

I'm one of those people who check the bank accounts every day. This is partly because I've been a victim of identity fraud not once, not twice, but three times, so I'm a bit obsessive about making sure every dollar is where it should be. (Have I mentioned I hosted a personal finance show for six years?) After the leap, I also obsessed because it's much harder to make assumptions about what you're earning and spending when there's nothing regular about your paychecks. I manage the household finances too, so I pay all the bills and track every dime that comes in and goes out. That doesn't mean I'm good with money. It just means I'm organized with it.

Some people might advise you to set aside, say, an hour or two each week (on your schedule!) to make sure all of your finances are in order, especially those related to your now-non-regular work payments. If that works for you, do it.

There are lots of services out there that help automate, or at least provide templates for, payables and receivables, and I find them much more convenient than trying to put together and format my own invoices. I use aynax.com for a very reasonable $9.95 a month. I also use Quicken, but I don't keep different books for my "business" because it's not necessary yet. If and when I start making megabucks, then maybe I'll invest in separate accounts. That would be fun!

When you're working for yourself, don't be shy about pestering people if they're not paying you on time. I'm extremely fortunate that I have yet to have a bad experience in this area, but I've heard horror stories, and if you find yourself becoming one of them, be as forceful as you have to be, and if worse comes to worst, get an attorney.

The Work Uniform

I mentioned above that I don't buy nearly as many new clothes as I used to. There is a school of thought in self-employment that says you should dress the way you would at any other office, and if you do, it will be easier to tell yourself you need to work. OK. If that works for you, go for it. I felt like a slob for a while during a period of time when I was wearing yoga pants and T-shirts for entire days, and I didn't even bother to wash my hair! Anyone who knows me will know this is (or at least was) *not normal* for me. You should by no means descend into sloth-hood, but there's a middle ground that can allow you to give your button-downs and slacks a break.

After a while, like everything else, you can relax into the idea that you don't have to wear a suit or other uniform in order to get work done. Whenever I'm back in a radio studio, of course I dress the part, and it's actually fun—feels like dress-up for a few days. But I don't feel guilty, because I'm comfortable while I'm working. I think my record was five days in the same yoga pants and hoodie sweatshirt and fuzzy slippers. You will never see a photo of it, but it was fabulous.

You Are Worthy

Figuring out your value on the open market is one of the biggest challenges you will face, unless you're in a position to figure it out before you leave your job. When you were an employee, you had a sense of what you were worth based on whatever your employer was paying you, but that amount of money doesn't mean much when you're out on your own. Because of the industry I'm in, when I became self-employed, I was so flummoxed by this question that I got myself a booking agent/attorney who handles all my negotiations for speaking fees and the like. (And because of her, I found out I was worth far more than I ever knew or would have expected.) Pretty much every industry has some mechanism people can use to find out what the competitive rates are for various talent and experience levels.

My best advice is to talk with people in your industry, decision-makers, and see what they're willing to tell you. Negotiation is not fun, and you will need a strong backbone to charge what you're worth. Multiple studies have shown that negotiation is particularly difficult for women. I highly recommend a book called *Women Don't Ask*, by Linda Babcock, if you want to learn more about how to do it well. One lesson I've learned the hard way: if you submit a proposal or an estimate and the response back is "That seems reasonable"—you're undercharging! You'll know that next time.

You also want to make sure, when you're figuring out what to charge for your work, that you factor in all of the aspects your old take-home paycheck covered that didn't involve cash money, including health care and retirement contributions.

Also, learn how to say no if you're being undervalued or low-balled. Obviously if you're desperate for income, a smaller-than-desirable paycheck is better than none at all. But people talk, and if you undercut yourself on one gig, it makes it harder for you to charge someone else more in the future. Don't be afraid to quote a solid price.

The Schedule

Early on, I made a schedule for myself because this is what you're supposed to do to keep yourself busy and on track. I outfitted my home office (former guest bedroom) with a whiteboard, and I wrote on it an hour-by-hour suggestion for what I should do each day from the time I got up. I was used to a daily rhythm, and I figured I could make myself live by a new one.

Maybe some people actually follow through on these types of schedules, but I didn't. Not at all. It was laughable. If you think there are distractions at work, wait until you start working at home—and I don't even have children to factor in. For a while I felt terrible about this, about my total inability to stick to a regimen, and I felt like I was flailing around every day even though I had that day written in (water-soluble) black marker on the wall right next to me. I'm a freaking grown-up, after all, and I've lived by schedules my entire adult life, so why should this be so hard?

It took me several weeks to figure out what was wrong. I finally realized that the construct of the American workday is just that—a construct. Even though my former workplace didn't track how many hours I spent in the office, and nobody ever questioned whether I spent enough time there, there was still an expectation that I would be there and that during the hours I was there, I would be working. Some days were busy, some weren't, but they lasted around the same number of hours no matter how much or how little I had to do.

You may have seen writer David Cain's 2010 essay' called "Your Lifestyle Has Already Been Designed," in which he eviscerates both the American work style and the consumerism that necessitates it. "As technologies and methods advanced, workers in all industries became able to produce much more value in a shorter amount of time. You'd think this would lead to shorter workdays. But the eight-hour workday is too profitable for big business, not because of the amount of work people get done in eight hours (the average office worker gets less than three hours of actual work done in eight hours) but because it makes for such a purchase-happy public. Keeping free time scarce means people pay a lot more for convenience, gratification, and any other relief they can buy. It keeps them watching television, and its commercials. It keeps them unambitious outside of work." Hard to disagree with that logic.

At home, though, nobody's watching. Nobody cares. As long as you get done what you need to get done, it doesn't matter what your hours are or when you put them in. It's frustrating at first because you don't have the usual construct of knowing when the day starts and when it ends, so it's hard to measure your own productivity. Eventually it becomes liberating. I'm not saying you should do nothing all day, but be realistic about how much time it should actually take you to complete a task. If that means you have eight hours of serious work to do, then you should get organized and get busy! But if the work that you need to do will take up only four hours in a day, for Pete's sake, take advantage of it and don't busy yourself the rest of the day with BS just so that you can feel ultra-productive. If you tie yourself to the nine-to-five schedule, all you're doing is wasting time and the opportunity to break free. Trust yourself. If you're like me, you'll eventually relax into it and find that instead of scheduling the dog walk, it's much nicer to go when you feel like you need some fresh air and want to stretch your legs. (Do give yourself reasons to get out of the house, or whatever work environment you're in, which is good advice even for those in a traditional work space.)

As I said, these are just some collected observations, the wisdom of which seems obvious to me now, but that I neither imagined nor thought about prior to my leap. Sometimes it's the small things that are confounding. And I can almost guarantee that at some point in your journey, you will find yourself thinking, "Well, this is how it's *supposed* to work," based on someone else's definition of what it's like to be self-employed. So when you see articles about how the top twenty most successful entrepreneurs in the world start every day at three in the morning, feel free to skim them, laugh, and then ignore everything you just read. Try building yourself a different schedule for each of two or three weeks and see which one feels right. If you have children, the complexity of this entire process is even greater, and you'll need to navigate all the other responsibilities that go along with being a parent. But I guess what I'm really encouraging you to do is to find out what works for you. The beauty of the leap is that you can make that determination for yourself without being a slave to the expectation of How Things Are Done. And I hope it helps to know that other people have been just as confused and tentative as you.

8.
MONEY
MONEY
MONEY

One thing I've heard over and over since my leap is, "Oh, you're so lucky you can do that. I could never afford it."

Well, neither could I, really.

People assume that with all the knowledge I had gained from hosting a personal finance show that I must've had a giant rainy day account to fall back on when I quit. Surely the woman who could explain collateralized debt obligations knew enough to garner herself a nice fat emergency fund. She told everyone else, practically every week, that the only way to have financial freedom is to have at least six months' salary saved up, if not more.

And yes, I absolutely knew all that. But did I practice what I preached?

No, I did not.

I admitted as much to listeners every once in a while. I told them that I too had been a slave to credit cards, so much so that my parents had to bail me out in my twenties. I too had gotten one of those infamous exploding mortgages back in the mid-2000s, and I too found myself living a lifestyle beyond my means, even with each passing salary bump. I admitted all that, in the spirit of keeping it real and relating to my listeners.

The problem is that those behaviors hadn't really changed by the time I quit my job. We still didn't have a giant savings account, and I still spent money I didn't have, even though our annual household income totaled nearly a quarter of a million dollars when I was working. We took very nice vacations, we bought things for our home, we ate out often (even though I love cooking), we had expensive cars (more important than your house when you live in LA), we made regular and not-small contributions to charities, and on and on. We also put money aside in our retirement funds, taking advantage of the match from both of our employers. But all in all, I couldn't even tell you where the money went. I tracked it—as I mentioned earlier, I'm obsessive about checking the bank account—but that didn't mean I was paying real attention to all the large and small money pits that were swallowing so much of our disposable income. It didn't seem like that big of an issue, because we both had our well-paying jobs, and those jobs weren't going anywhere, at least not that we could foresee.

Our lifestyle was/is hardly extravagant. But we did saddle ourselves with a giant mortgage when we bought a 1,400-square-foot home in 2004, just as the housing market frenzy was peaking. It was a heart-stopping amount of money on principle, but it wasn't outrageous for the neighborhood, and certainly not for Southern California. Still, it is vast understatement to say it was a financial stretch for us. Did I mention that we put nothing down? It was a normal thing back then, something called a "piggyback loan" by which the bank gave you a first mortgage for 80 percent of the purchase price and then a home equity line of credit (HELOC) for the other 20 percent. Everybody was doing it! I knew that because I had to explain piggyback loans to listeners who wrote in asking whether they were a good idea. I would explain what they were and that they weren't a good idea for everyone, but that if you managed your finances well, they could work. I didn't say that I had one, and a couple of years later I found myself explaining why those loans were helping to crash the economy.

When I quit, the mortgage was the biggest question mark. I did back-of-the-napkin math on our expenses and figured out that we could manage, just barely, to pay our bills on Dan's income alone. But our lifestyle would have to change radically until I got another job. I actually told myself—and *Marketplace* listeners reading this will find this admission incredibly rich in hypocrisy—that we could tap in to our retirement funds if we got desperate. If you never heard anything else on my show, you heard me say not to touch your retirement fund for anything. *Anything.* And yet I held in the back of my mind that those could be our emergency funds if things got really bad. That, and selling the house. Those were the fallback plans.

I was, of course, extremely fortunate that my husband made enough to keep the household afloat. But I started to worry about money immediately after getting my final paycheck. And, to be honest, I haven't really stopped worrying about it. After twenty-two years of having a steady salary, it is hard to adjust to the idea that I don't always know when the next check will come in. Entrepreneurs deal with this all the time, and they have other loans and startup costs to manage as well.

I also felt guilty putting the entire burden for our financial survival on my husband. Not only had I worked on salary my entire life, but for a good chunk of our marriage I had brought home more bacon. I was lucky to marry a man who was cool with that, who never felt threatened by my earning power. But now, it was all on him, and I felt terrible about that. I felt inadequate, like I wasn't pulling my weight anymore. At various intervals over the next couple of years, I would ask if it bothered him that I wasn't earning what I used to. He would generally look at me like I'd grown two heads. "Of course not," he would answer, "it's not even something I think about." I would ask every so often if he was worried about money. "You'll let me know if it becomes an issue, right?" he would ask in response, since I was in charge of the household accounting. I told him I would, and he'd shrug and say he wasn't going to make it a top-of-mind concern as long as it wasn't for me.

In fact he never brought up money at all, except to double-check, as my final day of work got closer to reality, that we'd keep the roof over our heads. By that time we were thirteen years into our marriage, and we didn't keep track of whose salary was paying for what bills (we combined all of our finances when we got married). When I look back, I'm amazed that we didn't talk more about it. I still ask him every few months or so if he was ever as worried as I was when I told him I was going to leave my job. "Nope," he has said each and every time. "I knew you'd figure it out. I knew you had skills and talents, I knew you had made a name for yourself, and that you would *want* to work, so I didn't have to be concerned that you'd sit around getting depressed. I'm pretty sure I had more confidence in you than you did at that point." He's never been more right. And I've always wished I had as much confidence in my own future as everyone around me seems to have.

But we didn't sit down and go over everything and talk about it, so I stewed in my own vat of worry by myself. It was very hard, psychologically, to stop receiving regular paychecks. It was also hard to realize that my freelance and solo-preneur income was so much less than what I'd been making. Of course our net worth says nothing about who we are, but it was still a rough adjustment. I struggled with the notion of letting my husband make more than I was making after so many years of my making more than he did. As I noted earlier, I don't think it's ever been an issue from his side of the equation—all he cares about is that we make enough together to pay our bills and enjoy our lives. But for me, it was a hidden badge of honor, because I grew up in an era where wives making more than their husbands was still unusual. It made me feel somehow powerful, even though pretty much nobody else knew any- thing about our finances (and most likely wouldn't have cared even if they did).

I watched the nosedive in the money entering our bank ac- count, and I felt like a slacker-loser who was suddenly a parasite in the household. I was really no different from our two dogs and two cats, who never do anything to earn their keep. (We've talked to them about getting going on their screenplays— everyone in LA has one—but so far, crickets.) To make it all especially painful, the awful recognition of what a hypocrite I really was, after six years in personal finance reporting, to not have my act together after telling everyone else how to get theirs on track was never far from my mind. It was a shameful realization to face how cavalierly I had managed our finances, something I'd been aware of for those entire six years but that I had never really acknowledged because it wasn't difficult to get the bills paid.

My concerns over whether my husband had even the fleeting thought that maybe I was lazy or didn't care about our financial issues stemmed in part from my own insecurities but also from the comments other people made about the selfish aspects of quitting when you're part of a family. About two months after I left my job, I did a call-in show with Minnesota Public Radio about quitting, and during the broadcast some guy named Jeff wrote in the comment area on their website: "This whole conversation seems like an 'eat, pray, love' fantasyland. . . . Someone still has to work in a relationship if one person quits. . . . Seriously, just take a year off to read books, make meals, and walk the dog? This is pure fantasyland that only college professors and wives or husbands who make a decent living can allow the other spouse to quit. Even then it seems like the 'quitters' are completely forgetting about the additional pressure that the working spouse feels about the normal bills . . . car, house, insurance, food, gas, water, electricity. . . . Those don't go away when you quit."

No, they certainly don't. (And there's that dismissive "eat, pray, love" reference again!)

But what I eventually realized, and what I want you to think about, is what is being gained when that second steady income is being lost. Yes, my husband and I had to make some sacrifices when I made my leap. We had to adjust our lifestyle. At the time I resigned, I believed that other things would come along, that other opportunities I had never been able to take advantage of before would now show themselves. That's where the faith part comes in, where I think the concept of a leap of faith becomes important. I would have known for sure if I had asked, but I had to believe my husband when he said he was OK with carrying the load for a while. At some points in our relationship he was making more than I was making, at other points I was making more than he was, and I think he was glad, actually, that his salary was enough that it made it possible for me to make this big life change.

Peg Streep points out that there is an "oversimplification [of quitting] in that most of us don't get to make these changes without giving up something else."

Exactly. You do have to realize before you do this that there are trade-offs. Some of them will be small, some of them will be huge. Many of those trade-offs will be financial. Yes, you should try to plan before you leap. Yes, you should prepare your finances. But when you have an uncertain timeline, it's hard to know just how much preparation is enough, and you can delay and delay and delay your leap while telling yourself that you need more of a cushion. Chances are you will have no idea how much is enough in terms of saving up for something like this. What's just as important is thinking about what you are willing to give up in the pursuit of happiness, fulfillment, curiosity, mental and emotional health, and all the other things that you will suddenly be able to attempt and experience when you have, in fact, quit.

And, in some cases, you either can't or you won't prepare before you leap. And you find a way to get through.

III

Adjusting your lifestyle is never easy. Millions of people were forced to do it during and after the Great Recession. And before you make a big career decision, it's worth going through the exercise to get a feel for what it will be like if you quit your job.

Todd Attridge spent thirty years working in the restaurant industry, starting as a fry cook at McDonald's and ultimately landing as director of operations for a national brand in Canada. When he wrote to me, he was up for a vice president position at his company:

"With only one problem—I hate it. The idea of going back to my job each day can, at times, be paralyzing because there's no personal fulfillment. [But] my career has partially defined me, and nobody but me can imagine me doing anything else."

He said he wasn't in a position to be able to just quit, as much as he wanted to do exactly that. So he told me later that he tried to find ways to make the job he was already in more palatable. "I don't know if you've ever been in that spot where you want to make it work. You're sort of hoping that you can fake it till you make it, right? And [everyone] is saying ooh look at you, you're at the top of the ladder, and I'm saying, 'Yeah, but I don't like it! I'm not happy!'"

Todd was in the audience, with his partner, Steve, when I gave my World Domination Summit speech. He told me later that it was the primary catalyst for him to make a change. "You finished talking, we walked out, Steve looked at me and said, 'You've got to get out of your job.' And I said, 'I've got to get out of my job. You're right. I've got to go.' And so that was the moment when I said, OK, I need an exit strategy. I need to get out of this and go back to the sweet spot, and how do I get there?"

I'm not going to take *all* the credit for inspiring Todd to take the leap—it wasn't a new discussion. They'd been talking about it for five to six months, on and off. On the plane back home from Portland, he made a list of six things he wanted to accomplish by the next summit, and one of them was "course correct my career." When he got back to work, he met with his boss and had an honest discussion about his feelings about his job. And in a remarkable bit of humanity, instead of freaking out, his boss said, "OK, go ahead and resign your position. Give me a couple of weeks' transition time, and I'll give you a package that makes it possible for you to go do what you want to do." (At which point I asked if I could go work for this person!) So about three weeks after getting back from the summit, Todd quit and started his own business teaching leadership skills, something he'd always been interested in doing.

Of course, the money question lingered. "At the end of the day," he said, "you might do what you want, but when the bank wants your house back, it sort of changes your outlook, doesn't it? So one of the things that we did was re-jig our finances to find out what was the least amount of money we needed to bring in as a household that would still allow me the latitude to do what I'm doing. As long as we have that covered, we're fine. That actually gave us some comfort, because we weren't far off from where we needed to be."

So Todd didn't have any idea where he would land and whether he would be able to truly make a go of this new business. There were no guarantees about anything, including income. And like me, he had to adjust his idea of where money fit in his definition of success, especially since he was now an entrepreneur.

"When I sat down, I actually tried to figure out how to monetize this. How do I take what I really want to do and turn it into money? And I started off really focused there—and I discovered I was . . . actually painting myself back into the same corner I had already been in, which was doing something I really didn't want to do but that I knew people would pay for. I did get to a moment where . . . I had to shake that and just say, 'OK, let me back up and really focus on what I want and make it about me for a moment. That's why I left that career in the first place.' I sat down and wrote tons about what's important to me, what do I believe in, and *then* I said, 'OK, so what will people pay for?' So there was a shift there."

III

Jim Wang experienced the shift as well, after several years of making a good living in the defense industry (radar development). Jim was on my radio show a few times when I did a series of stories about personal finance bloggers. He has a blog called *Bargaineering* where he gives advice to readers about how to manage their finances. That site became his full-time job once he leaped from corporate America.

"What if this is a flash in the pan?" he asked himself in an interview we did for this book. "It may do well now, but in a year, if it disappears, what's going to happen? Part of [the adjustment to that uncertainty] was getting over the idea that starting your own business is too risky. I mean, it's a common Asian stereotype. Why do you become a doctor, a lawyer? Because once you get there, it's relatively stable. [Turns out] no chosen career, even a high-profile and lucrative one, is always a pot of gold, but thirty years ago, everybody thought it was."

Jim started his work life in the defense industry, working first on radar development and then helping to design work-flow management tools. He was only a couple of years into his career when he started a travel website that he hoped would turn into something like Kayak or Expedia. But he couldn't devote that much time to it, so instead, he turned it into a personal finance website that did well almost immediately. He started wondering if he could turn that site into his new day job. "It was multiples of my [defense industry] salary. Like five or six times," he told me, "all through affiliate marketing. So it was almost a no-brainer. If I didn't do this, if I didn't make the full-time jump, I'd regret not doing it. You never know how long things are going to last."

Jim's leap wasn't into the vast unknown. He had an idea of what he wanted to do next, but, in 2005, website entrepreneurs like him weren't exactly a rare breed; still they were certainly not as prevalent as they are today. At that time, he might as well have been leaping into a void. He said the entire time he was contemplating it, all he could think about was that he was getting off the track that says when you grow up, you graduate, get a good job, work nine to five, and that supports you until you retire. And he kept reminding himself how far he already was in his career, even though he was only in his mid-twenties. "I had all the [national security] clearances that I would ever need to have a job for the rest of my life." But he decided he had to take the chance. And he realized that he could always go back and get those clearances again if the website didn't work out long-term.

What he didn't do is to leap without looking hard at his own financial status. It was natural, given the subject of his fast-growing personal finance website, to make sure that he had his proverbial ducks in a row. And that meant that he needed a clean bottom line before anything else. It's a caution every leaper should heed.

"We've become very good at owing people money," he said, "whether it's rent or a car payment or high-interest credit cards. You build up all these obligations. And companies also know this. Employers know this. And you build up all these expenses, and then it becomes a lot harder for you to test something on your own. The best time to test it is when you're twelve and you're living at home and have no expenses! But you get to that point where you are married, have kids, and most people cannot just drop everything and say, 'I'm going to try something new.' Because they have all these other obligations. That's sort of the idea of golden handcuffs that force you to stay because you can't see the path just jumping off that cliff."

The best thing to do is not take on so many financial obligations that they turn in to those handcuffs. And that's something you can start from day one of your adult life. You have to make that decision about what works in your life and in your budget and about how confident you are that you'll be able to bring in what you need to the household. Jim pointed out that you also need to be prepared for your financial benchmarks to change. And that means having an entirely new mindset about your income.

"Working is like being at the circus. When you work for someone else, it's like you do your show, you get paid, you get your food, then you go home. When you're in the wild, it's all on you, and you have to worry about where your food comes from. So it's a totally different mentality. You can't be a seal and bounce a ball out in the wild and expect sardines to come flying your way. You have to figure it out."

And that's a process you have to conduct very much on your own, along with your family.

III

No one but you, and perhaps your accountant, can decide whether leaping is a financially viable option. I've already talked about the common emergency fund advice—six months' of living expenses saved up for that surprise car repair or a layoff or whatever else comes your way. But here's another way to think about that fund, courtesy of my friend Meg Favreau of the personal finance website wisebread.com:¹ call it your F#*k-You Fund. The fund that allows you to give the middle finger, if not to your boss, then to the career that you've tired of, the job you just can't take anymore. I've also seen it called a Freedom Fund. I like the latter because it feels powerful. "Freedom" is heady promise, and there's an element of fight in it, which is how you'll probably be feeling if you get to the point where you're contemplating a jump.

Figure out what a fund like that might mean for you. Do some math on your finances to evaluate what you have stored up so far and how long it will take you to get to a level of savings that you can be comfortable with. Don't ignore it as an issue and go blindly into this experience. You have to be aware of both the long- and short-term effects of your leap.

That said, money shouldn't be the sole thing that keeps you from doing what you need to do for your health and sanity and well-being; if it is, figure out if there's a way to fix that issue. Take a hard look at your lifestyle. If you're on the household accumulation hamster wheel, look at ways to get off it. One of my favorite articles of the last year or so was in the *New York Times*, a piece called "Living with Less. A Lot Less."² In it, the author Graham Hill detailed his efforts to downsize his life, even though he is a multigazillionaire who made his fortune as a prototype Internet consultant in the mid-1990s. (He sold his company, SiteWerks, in 1998, and founded TreeHugger.com in 2003, which he then sold to Discovery. Now he runs LifeEdited .com.)

"We live in a world of surfeit stuff, of big-box stores and twenty-four-hour online shopping opportunities," he wrote. "Members of every socioeconomic bracket can and do deluge themselves with products. There isn't any indication that any of these things makes anyone any happier; in fact it seems the reverse may be true."

It's very easy to imagine that if you had as much money in the bank as Hill does, you wouldn't have a care in the world and would never have to work another day in your life. But a lot of economists and psychologists are studying the intersection of happiness and wealth these days, and their findings largely square with what Hill has said. A 2010 study in the *International Review of Economics*[3] found that the one way in which consumption positively affected happiness was when people were consuming experiences, like travel or concert tickets or piano lessons. These activities seem to be so rewarding because they create social connections. Consumption of durables, though—basically everything from gadgets and clothes to appliances and cars and beyond—are not significantly associated with happiness. And that's far from the only study to show this—it's a finding we covered over and over on *Marketplace*, as we talked people through how they could go about getting off the so-called hedonic treadmill, where we get a temporary thrill and sense of happiness from our purchases, but eventually we take those things, those purchases, for granted, and they are no longer special.

Yet everyone is bombarded each and every day with the message that it is our duty as consumers to buy, buy, buy, and it's a siren call that is very hard to ignore. And not just because of external messages like advertising. In early 2014, researchers released a study that showed we are hardwired to pursue what they called "mindless accumulation."[4] The experiments involved adult men and women conducting tasks in exchange for chocolate (yes, I did say adults, even though it sounds more like a perfect experiment for children!). They could earn as much chocolate as they wanted, but they couldn't take any of it with them when they left the lab. Even knowing they couldn't take it with them, the volunteers consistently overearned. A similar experiment, where the reward was a joke, prompted the same kind of overachievement, or overearning, despite the fact that volunteers couldn't "take it with them" when it was over. It may be in our DNA to constantly try to earn more than we can ever spend, even if that effort makes us unhappy and deprives us of other valuable commodities, such as leisure time.

All of this is to say that you shouldn't feel guilty about those shoes or those gadgets or those creature comforts that you work so hard to surround yourself with. But you can stop and think about how many of them you really need—and use. It might sound daunting, and somewhat unpleasant, to imagine living without those little luxuries. But my own experience tells me we can overcome that instinct, however innate it may be. It is not only possible but actually very likely that you can be happier with less—you just have to give it a real try.

I unwittingly took part in a sort-of experiment on myself about two years into my leap. My husband's employer put him on a project north of Los Angeles, in the coastal town of

Ventura, far enough away from home that he was given a corporate apartment to live in Monday through Thursday. At first, I protested. "I don't want to have to manage the household all by myself for most of the week," I whined, "and by the way, we will all miss you!" But this is part of the consulting lifestyle, and he didn't have a choice, unless *he* wanted to get a new job. Given my employment situation, that didn't seem like a great idea to pursue. So we sucked it up for a while, and I started making short visits to that apartment, instead of his having to drive home and back each week.

The apartment was small—about 600 square feet smaller than our house: a bedroom, kitchen, living room, and bathroom—in a classic apartment complex full of students from Ventura College. I hadn't spent any length of time in a town that small since leaving for college myself, and I had no intention of spending any time there other than weekends. But I discovered that I got more work done in this small place that was away from the commitments and distractions at home in Pasadena. I didn't know a soul other than Dan, and I kind of liked it. I'd go out almost every day with my hair piled under a baseball cap, no makeup, sometimes even a bit disheveled, and I didn't care. I missed my friends who weren't close enough to drop in or meet up for coffee or lunch, but I was surprised at how much I enjoyed having absolutely nothing and no one scheduled in my day except for writing and walking the dogs. Plus, Ventura is right off California's Highway 1, it has a gorgeous harbor and beaches, and it's a relatively quick drive to Santa Barbara and its nearby wine country. I started staying for longer periods of time, bringing our menagerie of animals with me, and getting cozy in the apartment. It was sparse, but I started to not care about that. The kitchen was barely equipped, but that forced me to get creative when I was cooking. It turned out I didn't really need half a dozen mixing bowls and three kinds of tongs. For some people, that will elicit a "Duh!" and perhaps an eye roll, but it was a realization that, for me, was about twenty years in the making.

I had about five days' worth of clothing, and I didn't care. And I didn't worry about all the things that needed to be done to our house—new roof, new chimney, rotted deck overhang, and so on—because I wasn't in it. I liked not having the active responsibility of homeownership, though we were still paying the mortgage. I stayed in Ventura for weeks at a time, and every time I came back home, I suddenly felt overwhelmed by all of our stuff. It's not like we're hoarders, and you would never walk into our home and say, "Jeez, they have so much crap!" But I felt oppressed by so many options when compared to the sparser lifestyle up north. I *felt* the difference. I realized that I had gotten comfortable with the state of real simplicity. Dan and I started talking about whether we might just sell the house and go back to apartment living. Rather than feeling as if we need to keep the house because it's what people our age do, we're reevaluating whether we genuinely enjoy it, and whether it's worth the sacrifices that we make in order to maintain the mortgage. We're not being driven out of a lifestyle we love but instead are making an honest and educated decision about whether we truly love it anymore. We had checked off the homeownership box, and now it might be time to move on.

I share this story because people always ask me how I've adjusted to having less money. Now, it's easy to say I'm good with downsizing when I had plan A (our house in Pasadena) sitting there waiting for us if we got tired of the apartment. I don't know what it would be like to spend months on end, or years, in what is a fairly cramped space for six living beings. But the experience forced me to confront my own long-standing consumption habits, and what I discovered was eye-opening. Our lifestyle has changed in big and small ways because of it. Time away from "regular" life taught me that maybe I could do with even less.

|||

The way we show progress in our society, the way we show what a great job we're doing, is by making more and more money. But if you think about this, it is a deeply flawed measuring stick. I so admire the people who work in charities and other places where, frankly, you work harder than most of the rest of us and get paid far, far less. Doing good for people is the marker of real success. It's a cliché, but it's true.

I've learned a lot since those early post-leap days. I'm now making about two-thirds of what I used to make, but I'm proud of the fact that I'm doing all of that on my own, generating the work for myself and in control of what I do and don't do. And I've also finally realized that, honestly, nobody else gives a crap what I make. So why should I? I put more pressure on myself than anyone else did, and I'm finally starting to judge myself not by the color of my Amex but the content of my character. I don't think I've ever been *obsessed* with wealth, but I certainly wanted to have the lifestyle I had during an upper-middle-class childhood. I wanted to do at *least* as well as my parents did, and the promise in this country has always been that you will do *better* than your parents. I think that promise is, unfortunately, dead because of how our economy now works. So maybe the pressure will let up, although the dreams never will. And they shouldn't. But I've stopped looking at my paychecks as some sort of indication of my own value, and that's a psychological change that I never would have predicted two years ago.

Do what you need to do, and what leads to the best life, for you and your family. Look around and think about what you can do without. It's more freeing than you realize. Take small steps at first—you don't have to move into a small apartment!—but start with getting rid of multiples of things you have. You might find that you're happier with less, especially when less allows you to take your Freedom Fund and never look back.

9.
THE KIDS WILL PROBABLY BE ALL RIGHT

Now that we've established that I made gigantic financial mistakes in this whole process and didn't plan at all as I should have/was supposed to/would have advised myself on the radio, let's get to the other reason that many people love to trot out when they tell me they could never just up and quit without a plan: "The only reason you can do this is because you don't have kids."

I do not have children, and that is by design. Many of the people I spoke with for this book also came from households where diapers, school supplies, and college funds were not an issue, because they too did not have kids. And according to the latest U.S. census report, they reflect the majority of the population. Nearly 60 percent of American households do not have children.[1] In fact, more homes have dogs than have children (and let me tell you, kibble ain't cheap!).[2] But kids aren't the only consumers of financial resources. Many households struggle with the needs of other dependents, from elderly parents to siblings-in-need to other loved ones whose needs become our responsibilities.

When I left my job without knowing what came next, I was lucky in that I had only two people to worry about, two people who would feel the direct impact of my actions: my husband and me. That's it. So the math was pretty simple. Could we live on his salary, with adjustments to our lifestyle, and hopefully some freelance and project income from me? Could we keep a roof over our heads, chicken and beer in the fridge, and the all-important wet food for the cats? Yes. Would it be difficult? Potentially. Were the stakes high? It sure felt like it, but our lives weren't on the line. We didn't have anyone else relying on us for their continued existence.

What if, however, you have kids or parents who rely on you financially, or maybe even a sister who regularly crashes at your place whenever she loses a job? That's a whole different set of considerations. When you are responsible for other people, the idea of quitting because it's what's right for *you* is anathema to the very idea of being a good person. It probably feels selfish. And foolhardy. And beyond imagination. Feeding four mouths costs a lot more than feeding one or two. We all have heard the nightmare stories of what college costs now and is going to cost for today's kids. We know that aging parents haven't adequately prepared or saved for retirement, and adult children feel a natural obligation to help out, sometimes covering the entire cost of housing and food and everything else. So, yeah, quitting without knowing what you're going to do next? Selfish and foolhardy.

Except when it isn't.

Sibyl and Rob Chavis live in Pasadena, California, not far

from me, though I didn't know them prior to Sibyl's contacting me about my book project. They're both in their late thirties and have two young children.

If you looked up *ambition* and *success* in *Webster's*, you wouldn't be surprised to find Sibyl and Rob listed in the definitions. Both graduated from Harvard Law School, and then they both got jobs at the largest legal firm in Atlanta. Both grew up in middle- to upper-middle-class environments that emphasized the need to succeed and find happiness. Sibyl's family, especially her mother, urged an advanced degree but also told her it was important to be passionate about her work.

"We were one of the few African American families in my neighborhood," she told me. "And so that in and of itself, I think, added a different dimension to the expectations of my parents, because you have to always make certain that you are essentially defying the stereotype and what people want to think about you because of your race. . . . I think I was conditioned to really make sure I fit into a certain box that took into consideration my race, the environment I lived in, and the expectation that it didn't matter what I did, but I needed to be successful at it."

She watched hour upon hour of *The People's Court* and decided she wanted to be an attorney, and so that's exactly what she became.

Rob, who didn't spend quite as much time with Judge Wapner,[*] had other aspirations. "I think I'm just a . . . I'm a rule follower in a lot of ways. It was, go to school, get good grades, go to college, get a job. I think for a long part of my life, I wanted to be president. So once that's your goal, everything else seems easy. I truly believed I could do anything I wanted.

So for a little while I wanted to be a doctor until I figured out you have to actually like science, then I bailed on that. I'm big on just keeping as many doors open as possible and moving into whichever one feels right at the right time."

So both of them arrived on the fast track after law school. And it was a life that anyone watching from the outside would have assumed was as close to perfect as it could be.

"Everyone wants to be here," Sibyl told herself, over and over, even as she started to realize she was tiring of her career. "Everyone wants to be sitting here. Well, not everyone, but a lot of people want to be here at this law firm. Be grateful! Everybody wants that paycheck! You're paying your student loans. You're driving the car you want. You're living in the condo you want. All of the pieces, Sibyl, you've done it. Woohoo! Check mark, check mark. I'm lining up my life because, by forty, I'm going to be retired on Easy Street, and I'm putting in my time now. I was lining up what I thought I was supposed to be, and that was going to have the payoff not only financially but emotionally."

"For me," Rob told me thoughtfully, "getting to a law firm just wasn't as stimulating as I thought it was going to be. I realize now, in hindsight, the fact that I got tired at work at three o'clock in the afternoon just meant I wasn't engaged. I didn't really have a plan to go do something else, but it just wasn't fulfilling me in the way that I thought it would. But I showed up every day; I stayed as long as I was supposed to; I did my work; I turned it in, and it was good."

Not only was the work good but it gave Rob and Sibyl the ability to surround themselves with the classic outer trappings of success. Everybody saw how well they were both doing, and that made it harder to acknowledge that maybe they weren't as happy as they felt they should be. "We were twenty-four, getting six-figure checks. How is anybody going to tell me I'm not successful? There are lots of people who never make that amount of money in a single year, and this is my first job."

But the pressure was always on to pursue that next rung on the success ladder, to keep making more and more money, and to work harder.

People make so many assumptions about your success based on outward indicators like what kind of house you own, what kind of car you drive, what your title is at work, how long you've been there, the kind of work you do. It is rarely based on whether you feel successful and fulfilled. I'm fortunate that I both loved my job and happened to work in an industry with an external cachet. For many successful people, job satisfaction is missing from the equation, even if they have all those other things.

Sibyl and Rob spent the next decade as in-house counsels for an ad agency just outside Detroit. They enjoyed more of the traditional trappings of success Sibyl talked about. But Rob told me they started to feel like they were just doing another lap around the track, even though this job brought new and different challenges. It wasn't exciting or fulfilling anymore. But what else would they do? They were good at their jobs, they had specialized skills, and they were being rewarded for their hard work.

"The number one thing that kept coming up in my mind was, 'But we have children!'" Sibyl said. "If it were just us, we would have gotten an apartment, eaten ramen, kept our expenses really low. But we didn't feel like we could do that and live up to the commitment we had made to our kids. So that meant that while we could cut back on a lot of expenses, there were others we couldn't. I still had to pay my daughter's tuition and pay for the other things she wanted to do. She would say to us, 'I don't care what you two crazy people have done. I want to go to camp!'"

In 2011, for reasons both practical ("tension within our working environment") and philosophical ("I feel like I've done the corporate America thing"), they hit a point where they felt like their situation had to change. Sibyl was pregnant, and their first child was about to enter kindergarten. They worried that they didn't have enough money saved to just up and quit together, but they felt as if they couldn't just wait for the perfect time for that to happen either.

Sibyl told me that she and Rob comforted themselves with the idea that they could live off their savings to ensure that the kids had a smooth transition until things settled down in their new life.

"The only thing they should know is that Mommy and Daddy are happier, and they're spending more time with them—because we're unemployed!" she said, with a laugh. Most people don't laugh when they talk about the potential for unemployment, but if there is such a thing as an eternal optimist, it's Sibyl. For better or for worse, she believes in her bones that things will turn out all right. And she was confident, at that moment of decision, that the ledger for them was more skewed to the pro side of the pros-and-cons list. It may be easier to just stick with what you're doing and stay the course, she said, but that just didn't feel right to them.

They quit their jobs and moved to Los Angeles. Two lawyers

with one kid and another one on the way, in 2011, three years into a recession that was wreaking havoc on the U.S. economy.

Sibyl wanted something of a time-out in her career track, and she wasn't sure what she wanted to do next. Rob had a better idea of what he wanted to do. He loves comedy, and he loves writing. He started a blog where he wrote about whatever was in his head, and he started to get an audience for his writing.

"For me," said Sybil, "it was going to be a way to get even more involved in my daughter's activities, because I had been a working mom from nine to six or seven o'clock at night. With this leap, I got to go to two o'clock cheerleading performances. And I started understanding that freedom and my being able to go after something I was passionate about. I understood that with my being happy and Rob's being happy, our children would be able to see us living what we believed. They would see that we did take a chance, but we were thoughtful about it, and we worked really hard to create this new life and new careers."

For Sibyl and Rob, as with pretty much anyone else who leaps without a net, it was a leap of complete faith. The way they see it, living with uncertainty means you are far more open and flexible to take advantage of opportunities that come your way that you otherwise would be too busy, too tied up, to inside-a-plan, to jump on. And it's not like you lose your foundation. You don't lose the skills you already have, and unless you're away from them for years on end, they're not likely to atrophy over a span of a few months.

Sibyl has said that she has basically trained herself to live in the moment, or at least in the day, and she has tried to let go of the fear that pervaded any thoughts of the future, because she found it counterproductive to invest all that worried energy. Sound like magical thinking? Well, maybe some of it is. But it's tempered by reality. "If you put your fears on the board—fear of giving up your career, fear of not having enough money, fear of people thinking you're crazy, fear of going after something and people seeing you go after it and seeing it not work out, fear of not really knowing how to get to where you want to be—if I had all those fears up there, I would say 95 percent belong in the money category. If it weren't for that fear, then people would leave their jobs all the time. And the money fear is in your face every day. You gotta go pay for something. Even signing on to my bank account would cause anxiety because there's so much going out and nothing coming in. But that again is just another fear that has to be worked through."

So, how did she train herself, and Rob, to live in that moment and get through the fear? She does something she calls "mindset pushups." Each day, the moment she wakes up, while she's still in bed, she rates her emotions on a scale of 1 to 10, with 10 being happy and motivated. With that number in mind, she starts off the day listening to maybe some classical music and mentally checking off whatever fears have cropped up in her head. "Well, maybe it's that I'm going to run out of money," she told me. "OK, what does that mean? Then I have a rational conversation with myself that, you know what, it's not going to happen. It's going to work out, and the reality is if you needed to, you could just go try to get a job. You're fine." She also keeps a what's-already-working list. Every time something positive happens, it goes on that list, and before she writes up a daily to-do list, she spends time looking over that other list of what's already working. She's also a part of the wider mindfulness movement that promotes quiet time, meditation, deep breathing, and the like, and she says she basically talks herself through the days. "I'm very disciplined about it. So is Rob. You have to overshadow your own doubts. This is where I feel that I have developed a muscle. It's no different than any other muscle you have to develop. It's there. It just needs to be strengthened."

Rob agreed. "For me, even if the path isn't clear, I feel much better today waking up and working hard and heading forward in some direction than being at times where I was before when I was just flipping the same switch every single day and not really moving forward. I don't live my life based on a guarantee, because I don't buy it. Anything can happen. A lot of times we think, 'Oh, yeah, if I do it like this and I do it like that and I go to work every day and it's secure and safe, then I can protect my little world and everything is good.' The reality is we've seen that guarantee blown up on so many different occasions from people who are 'not taking any risk.'"

This is a refrain I heard over and over from people who have leaped, with or without children—that there is a false sense of security in sticking with what you know. After all, if the 2008 financial crisis proved anything, it's that no amount of experience, loyalty, or employee value keeps people from losing jobs they thought they'd have forever. Talk all you want about the risk of leaving something you think is stable, but sometimes the risk itself is in staying, because you don't expose yourself to other possibilities and opportunities. And that can make you even more vulnerable if a job loss comes involuntarily.

I ran into Sibyl a few months later at a local Starbucks. She told me Rob had gotten a job as a writer for a new NBC sitcom.

She had asked Rob how much money he would be bringing into the household budget, and he said he wasn't sure. He hadn't done the math to figure out what that would be after agents' and lawyers' fees. Not that they didn't care or didn't have concerns about where the next paycheck was coming from, but they didn't linger over it as an issue. She laughed in disbelief, but she said they *still* weren't worried about making it work. And a couple of years into their big leap to California, the kids were doing just fine.

"This is the thing," she said. "I think when you sign up for children, you sign up to jump in your safety net if you have to. And at the end of the day, Rob and I are both attorneys. We had careers, and we had experience. If I got to the point where my children weren't eating, they weren't feeling provided for, or they could not go to the school that they would have been able to because of the decision I made, I would go back to work. Whatever it took, I would do. So while right now I'm pushing it and doing it this way, if the time comes and Jordan is seventeen, and it's time for him to go to college and we're in a position where we can't pay tuition, I'd work anywhere. I would do whatever I needed to. I'm resourceful enough that I could get a job."

There's no guarantee of that either, of course, but they're confident that because things have worked out so far, they'll get through, no matter what.

"You know, a couple of years ago when we both quit," Sibyl added, "I would say our faith-to-fear ratio was about 50-50. We'd have times when we just let it go and trusted that something good would happen, that we'd make it happen. And we'd have times where it was really uncomfortable and we did worry. Now, I'd say it's about 85-15 in favor of faith. Because it's worked."

I I I

For some leapers, there is a singular life event that prompts change. It might be a marriage or a birth. It might be something that happens to a close friend. For Aaron McHugh and his family, it was a death.

Aaron, his wife, and their two children live in Colorado Springs, Colorado. He and his wife celebrated their twentieth anniversary in December 2013.

For Aaron, quitting was the only way to truly break from the pain of an extraordinarily difficult, and drawn-out, family tragedy.

Aaron's career motivation was simple from the time he entered the workforce. Growing up, his family was, as he put it, of minimal means, and things got much tougher after his parents divorced when he was twelve. For the better part of his young adulthood, they lived, in part, off of food stamps.

"So I knew what I didn't want my life to look like, and you know . . . really, to be honest, it was shame avoidance . . . from beat-up cars to hand-me-down couches to hand-me-down clothes to all that stuff that goes with that. My first job was flipping burgers at McDonald's, and the major motivation for doing that was to buy my own clothes so that people couldn't tell how poor I was. And we weren't poor in terms of the world poverty level, but in terms of American poverty standards, we were on the scale. I had one pair of jeans and one pair of shoes and no socks, and so early on I said to myself, 'I'm not living like this.' It was just kind of the fire in my belly of knowing what I didn't want to do so I'd better figure this out myself."

He went to Baylor University in Texas, but he barely scraped by, grade-wise, and he left with a communications degree but no idea what to do with it. He married his college sweetheart, they moved to Colorado, and he worked at minimum-wage jobs for several years, including selling backpacks and tents at a local outdoor equipment store. Eventually, a friend pointed him to a position in radio and television advertising sales. "We were four months pregnant at the time, and the advertising job came with health insurance so I said sure, OK, I'll give it a try," and he stayed in that line of work for nearly ten years. After that, he moved into software sales, and he has been there ever since. He's now in his early forties.

The year he transferred into a new industry—software— they had their second child, Hadley, who was born without all of her brain.

Doctors told the family when Hadley was four months old that she would probably never walk, talk, go to college, get married, or have any semblance of a normal life.

"He just went down this list, and my wife and I were feeling like, What? Whose life is this? I just didn't even know what to do. So career-wise, immediately one of the things the doctor said was, 'Do not ever go one day without health insurance. If you do, you will live in your parents' basement, and you'll be bankrupt, and you will never recover.' What I took from it was, OK, for the rest of my, career I'd better play it safe."

I was dumbstruck as he told his story. I literally could not imagine what their lives were like with a child who needed every moment of their care and attention. Their daughter never walked or talked, she was tube fed and wheelchair bound, and she had cerebral palsy and seizure disorders. It was a crushing amount of stress while trying to keep a marriage and a family together. They also had a third child.

"So, for a career during those years," he said, "to be really frank, it was just keeping my sh*t together, just going to work, making sure I didn't flub it up. I might have had dreams and visions and desires, and a lot of people around me started doing some remarkable things, and I wasn't feeling so remarkable. I knew I had the DNA to play ball in the big leagues, and it was really, really tough to just sit back and play on the farm team because I wasn't able to take promotions or move to different city if I even wanted to or go work for this entrepreneurial startup and risk not getting a paycheck. I had great experiences at the software company, but in my right mind, I would have never stayed that long."

Hadley died when she was twelve. It was an unbelievably crushing blow to the family. But what it also meant, Aaron said softly, was that they were able, for the first time in twelve years, to look back and realize what they had just lived through. "In the middle of war you just don't have a lot of time to process. The real, true weight of all of it hadn't caught up to us." It was also the first time in twelve years that they could look at their lives and think about what they *wanted* to do rather than what they *had* to do.

The family spent the next year "just showing up," as Aaron put it. Eating. Sleeping. Processing.

"And after that first year, it became really, really clear that, wow, OK, I have some freedom of choice now. Personally I've always been really driven—climb mountains for fun and do triathlons, Ironman, and marathons—and when I just didn't have the wherewithal, it really helped notch things down and helped me make an assessment of what I was doing. What am I doing these things for? Which things am I doing just to try to cope with my life, which things do I actually love, and which things do I really want? What are the ingredients we want in our life? So part of what I started doing was asking, Who am I? What am I good at? And why does it matter?"

These are important questions, and if it takes a major life change to prompt you to start asking them, then fine. But it's also fine not to wait for that moment and to start asking them right now.

At the urging of friends, Aaron started blogging about his experience and about the soul-searching he was doing for himself. He started to feel stronger as people reacted to his story. It gave him a confidence that he didn't even know he had lost, and he started talking about quitting his job. His wife told him she was tired of seeing him be miserable, and she gave her blessing to the idea. When he resigned, coworkers asked whether he'd won the lottery, or if a grandmother had passed away and left a bunch of money. "I realized," Aaron told me, "what it comes down to is that the concept of jumping without a net is so absolutely foreign that it doesn't make any sense to people, so there must be a problem." He told them that, no, he hadn't won the lottery, but he had saved enough that he could take some time away and reevaluate his career priorities.

As for the financial aspects of quitting even though he had a family to support, Aaron said that of course he had worried. "That was number one, no question." But because of the advice he'd heard on the radio show of personal finance guru Dave

Ramsey—advice to have a so-called emergency fund equal to three to six months of living expenses—Aaron and his wife had started building up just such an account several years earlier. They didn't call it an emergency fund, though, or a savings account. They called it a "liberation account."

"I wanted to be able to be in a conference room, or in a meeting," said Aaron, "and if it got bad enough, I could just stand up and leave. Just hand in my pink slip on the way out of the driveway. At one point, I couldn't do that because I had people in tow. I had kids and a wife and everything that goes with that. And we were already living below our means. But we slowly plugged away at [the savings goal we had set], and as soon as I got to a place where I had four to five months' worth of pay in that liberation account, it meant we had a huge piece in place in our preparation to consider a jump." In addition to that account, Aaron and his wife sat down and made a list of all the things that could go wrong—a Murphy's law list of sorts. "We said, OK, how bad could it get? Here's the liberation account, and, well, what if we burned through that? And then burned through our retirement fund? And what if we went all the way down to the worst case: move in with my brother in his basement. And I could get a job with the company I used to work for fifteen years ago. And then I wrote, OK, if it got that bad, would it still be worth it? And I thought, 'Yeah, I'm that miserable.' I'd burn it all even if it meant that's what it would look like."

They sat down to talk with their kids, who, at the time Aaron decided to leap from his job, were seventeen and eleven years old. The only questions the kids asked him were whether they would still get allowances and whether they could keep their membership to the local swimming pool. "I said, yes, I'll find a way. Once we did it though, they were excited because I was around and available!"

A few months later, however, both kids went to him, privately and on separate occasions, and asked whether things were still OK. They wanted to make sure that the family wasn't going to run out of money. They told their dad that it didn't make sense that he wasn't going to work and yet the family was still able to pay the bills. "They just saw that all of their friends lived better than we did—cars and vacations and stuff in their house. We told them that we had chosen not to have that stuff because we didn't want to be hostage to it. I felt bad for them because I could tell they were just uncomfortable, uncertain, and I just said, 'Guys, you know what? It has to get really bad for a really, really, really long time for you to have to worry about whether or not we can afford to stay in our house."

That was a decision that Aaron and his wife had made, unrelated to his leap, to keep expenses down and "stuff" to a minimum. "I would love a new car with leather seats, but not as much as the freedom to say I'm not coming to work tomorrow. I think what happens, in my opinion, is that people talk all day long about what they want their life to look like, but very few put that into actionable steps, and then they just bellyache about how their life doesn't look like they want it to. You have to craft your life in such a way that it makes it possible."

You can't leap and expect that there will be no pain. And you can't leap and assume that your life will continue the way it's always been. You have to know that there will be sacrifices and there will be changes. You will have to make choices, especially when it comes to the money stuff. Of course, everyone's financial picture is different, and this kind of leap, unless you've won the lottery or amassed millions in the bank, is never easy. But Aaron believes—as I do—that fear plays just as big a part as finances do in the decision to quit. After he told me about the list he had made of worst-case scenarios, I told him I still wasn't sure how that made him feel comfortable with leaping and how he got over that psychological hurdle that tells you everything could fall apart at any minute if you take this kind of risk.

"I think for me, honestly," he answered, "because we lost our daughter, one of the things I felt like was, in my life— and I've heard similar feelings expressed by people who've gotten divorced and experienced other hardships—OK, the worst thing has already happened to me. And I survived. So if I can survive that, then everything I could imagine that could be terrible would not be as terrible as that."

III

After leaving his company, Aaron started consulting within his industry, and he found out that he could earn more money in two days of work a week than he did with a full-time job. "It was hilarious, 'What?! Nuh-uh!' What did I wait so long for? What was I so afraid of?" He has since found a new full-time job, with a fancy VP title and compensation to go along with it. But he's working a lot and, despite enjoying the work, he expressed some wistfulness for the part of the journey that allowed him to both test his abilities as an entrepreneur and spend more time with his family.

But more than anything, he says, he looks back on his leap as the time when he finally figured out his priorities. And there's no doubt his kids were watching every step of the way, and hopefully they learned from his experience. "I just found that so much of this story of jumping," he said, "really comes down to what you want in life. What do you want? And you have to get really, really clear on that. Do you want stuff? Do you want to travel? Relationships? What do you want? Most people jump because there's something about their circumstance that they don't like or something that is not gratifying or satisfying, or is super difficult. So in the course of living through that, because you're forced to really get inside your head and your mind and your heart, you can get real clear before you take a leap." In addition, he says, that list he made of worst-case scenarios was accompanied by a list of what became important to him in his life, a list that included what he was or was not willing to tolerate in a work environment, and a list of things he wanted to see happen in his daily life, including taking his kids to school. And he vows to carry those lists through any and all other transitions he makes in his career.

"I'm now committed to doing this again every time I change jobs. I will never quit on Friday and show up at a new job on Monday. It's a crazy thing that we do. You quit, and you don't have any time off, because you don't want to miss a paycheck. Now I'm committed to taking three to four months off every time I'm done with a gig. I'll burn through my savings if I have to just so that I can live and rest and play and live my life. Because work's always going to be there."

I'm willing to bet his kids are perfectly happy with that promise.

10.
NOT ALL PEACHES AND CREAM

The Chavises, the McHughs, and many other leapers I talked with did good amounts of planning before they walked away from the careers they'd built. But then there are those like me who did not do that kind of planning, certainly not to any great extent. I've spent part of this book saying that you can still survive and thrive if you do it that way, and I'm not the only example of it working out. But I also thought of subtitling the book "Sewing Your Parachute on the Way Down," because you have *got* to start thinking and working fast to make your leap worthwhile. It's important to be realistic about what failure looks like so that you can be ready for it if, in fact, plan B doesn't show up, or isn't the right one, and you need to move on to plan C or D or beyond. Because plenty of people will tell you that leaping without a net is *not* a good idea, and you should hear from at least a couple of them.

First, David Sobel. All you really need to know about David is the title of a piece he wrote for Salon.com: "I Never Should Have Followed My Dreams."

"Changing one's career in a tight economy," he wrote, "without the proper pedigree of internships and connections, was like trying to audition for a pop band in midlife without an instrument. [. . .] Broke and ashamed, I asked my parents for money and tapped my 401(k) to make my COBRA payments. I'd believed that resigning at forty-two was my acknowledgment of unrealized potential. Now I thought it was the delusional move of a man child who'd missed out on the party."[1]

Oh dear. Well, that's not really all you need to know about him. David is forty-three and lives in Manhattan. He's a sax player and always figured that would be his career calling, but as we all know, that kind of life is hard to come by. After college, where he majored in jazz performance, "I kind of fell into this temp life of doing a lot of word processing," he told me. "I knew I had an artistic streak in me, but I just didn't have the guts to follow it."

By his mid-thirties, David was in a job where, as he puts it in his piece, "I'd sit in a windowless office and format reports in Microsoft Word," but he couldn't tolerate what he says was a hostile work environment. He left in March 2013, without having another job lined up, and decided to try to launch a writing career. He's been trying ever since, and it's been difficult, to say the least.

"When I quit I was working at a nonprofit and not making a lot of money," he said. "My parents helped me, because I was looking for jobs and wasn't getting anything and it got very desperate. It was horrific. I went into severe depression and thought I had destroyed my life. I just couldn't believe I couldn't even get a temp job. I had recruiters telling me, 'Well, you don't even have administrative skills.' And I would say, 'What do you mean, I'm a master of Word and PowerPoint and

Excel, what other administrative skills are there?' And one guy said, 'You don't have experience "calendaring,"' as if that was brain surgery. And every time that happened it was just horrible, because I know I'm a very intelligent person and that I can do things if someone would just give me a chance. It was really a hard time."

For more than a year, Sobel tried for temp jobs while writing, and that didn't work out. He says he couldn't even get a job at Starbucks.

He has certainly soured on the power of positive thinking, and I don't blame him. There is no guarantee that things will work out the way you hope that they will, no matter how much unrealized potential you have. David says he believes that today's economy makes it impossible for workers to take risks like the one he did. I'd push back that it's not impossible, but it is certainly challenging. Middle-class wages and salaries have not kept up with inflation and the cost of living; housing is supremely expensive, especially in coastal states; small business loans to follow up on any entrepreneurial urge are not handed out like candy; and there is incredible competition for creative jobs, including those that live online and allow you to work from home. And yet the drumbeat from business and self-help books alike is that taking risks will always be rewarded and will pay off in the end. Unfortunately, that's just not true.

David wanted nothing more than to be a writer, and that's all well and good and something I can relate to. But it's important to think about what you want to do, what you're already good at, and how hard you're willing to go after it before you take that leap of faith. I knew I loved talking to people and spreading information and doing that in a high-profile way, and I had experience that proved I was capable of those things. I was willing to work really hard to figure out a way to use those skills again. In hearing David's story, and still empathizing with his disappointment, I nevertheless found myself wishing he had done some deeper experimenting before his leap, working into a new identity as Herminia Ibarra talked about in Chapter 2. I'm totally with him that the Happy Talk around career reinvention can be full of promised riches and contentment that is not grounded in the reality of the economy and the workplace. But leaping is hard work, and nobody owes you anything—something I learned after waiting and waiting for my own phone to ring with offers from hundreds of national media outlets. If you don't want to hustle or face rejection multiple times, leaping may not be a viable path for you.

The "follow your passion" job still hasn't appeared for David, but the day after we talked, he went back to work as a temp. He said he wasn't thrilled about it, but "at least I won't be sitting in a room alone."

III

Russ Kendall isn't a cautionary tale himself—he actually *did* follow his passion, right into a career running his own pizza company. Before that? He was an award-winning photojournalist and editor at the *Bellingham Herald* in Washington State, and the author of eight photography books for kids. But he's watched as plenty of his colleagues lost their jobs in recent years, and he's now on a mission to get everyone who's still left thinking about a plan B.

Several years ago, when he was in his early fifties, Russ

saw the writing on the wall—or, I suppose in his case, the photos on the wall. There'd been eight pay cuts already, and more pain was undoubtedly on the way. It had been happening for years in all corners of the news business, and his paper was no exception. He figured sooner or later his name would show up on a list of layoffs. In addition to the threat of downsizing, he didn't like the direction the paper was taking in its news coverage. "I don't mean to ring my own bell, but I'm pretty good at photo management, editing, design, and coaching, and I enjoy working at a fairly high level," he told me. "But at the *Herald*, by the time I finally jumped, I was embarrassed by the quality of the work I was doing. I saw staff who spent most of their careers fighting for photo respect get laid off one at a time. And to watch reader-submitted pictures of cute kids replacing hard-driving, meaningful journalism—it just got hard and harder. My blood pressure was off the scale, and it was basically, 'Hello, your heart attack is waiting for you in the hallway.'"

He'd already started a side business making pizzas to sell at the local farmers' market, partly because of those pay cuts he was dealing with. When his wife was offered a job she'd been pining for for years, they knew the only way she could take the job was if he transitioned into being more of a stay-at-home dad for their then eight-year-old son. The plan B was already in place (the pizza side business that he mostly did on weekends), he really wanted to leave a job he no longer relished, and the timing of all this seemed to work out for everyone. So he left photojournalism and started a catering business that he says pays better than his newspaper job ever did. He's sold close to ten thousand pizzas in two years. "You know, the universe may have been opening some doors for us, but if I hadn't started my plan B, it never would have happened. I remember at the first farmers' market, I sold thirty-five pizzas, and I was exhilarated and terrified. I burned a lot of them, and the lines were long. Well, now I cook seven at a time, and the line is even longer. I had to figure out how to learn these new skills, just like learning digital after film as a photographer."

In 2014, feeling "ever-greater heartsickness" over all the layoffs that continued to plague his former industry, Russ started a Facebook page for fellow journalists and photographers called "What's Your Plan B?" The cover photo on that page reads as follows:

> WARNING! The following photo gallery may contain images that could prove thought-provoking to those viewers who need constant reassurance that the world is a safe and cuddly place where they and their magic ponies can live undisturbed by any reference to Reality.

He started with a group of about fifteen friends, and it quickly grew into the thousands. "I'm just trying to get people to think about it," he said. "Just think about it! One of the hardest things for us journalists to do is to consider a world where we aren't doing journalism anymore. It's almost like a hostage situation. If I just keep my head down, they won't fire me; they'll take somebody else. And then you're a little bit relieved, but you also have survivor's guilt and you're working five, six days a week and then coming home and trying to decompress. You can tell yourself you don't have time to get a plan B organized and going."

The page encourages members to share their own plan Bs and suggestions for how to figure out what's next. I love that it encourages people to start doing groundwork early, so that when it comes time to leap, the parachute is already sewn— and even tested! Career gurus have been saying this for years, but it's cool to see it happening in these peoples' lives right there on the Facebook page. (And I always say that I'd much rather take advice from "real people" over gurus pretty much any day.) This way, you have not only a dream but part of a plan in place that includes gaining experience in what you've decided to pursue. And I don't think that's anathema to leaping without a net either—you can still do that without knowing exactly *where* you're going to land, but at least with some idea of where it might be *safe* for you to land.

I shared my leap story with Russ and asked what he thought about going through this kind of transition without a net, and he kindly told me, "Sure, if it worked for you, that's great. But if you have a family to support and you leap, there's some reality to what's going to happen, and I think there's a lot more pressure on you to figure out the next thing. My point is why not think about it? Think about what you love to do, what your skills are. Journalism is such a passion, and we invest so many years and decades of our lives into thinking that's what we are, but we're more than that. We're cooks, we're teachers, we're poets, we're mechanics, and by thinking about the possibilities before you get that call to meet your boss and HR in ten minutes, you're in better shape to deal with that."

▌▌▌

For many of us, plan B was incredibly hard to imagine. Whether we loved what we were doing, honestly couldn't picture anything else, or found the notion of starting something from scratch too overwhelming, there are probably more people who leap the way that Dave did than the way that Russ did. Most of the people I spoke with had a yearning to take a step back and really think and mull over what that next step should be. Some couldn't do, or didn't want to do, that thinking in the midst of their current job. Dave is right that our country isn't set up to make leaping easy for people, and I'd be the first one to tell you that this is hard work. But just because it's hard and scary and confusing at times doesn't mean that it's not worth doing. For me, at least, the lack of a net has completely changed the experience of career transition, I'd argue, for the better. It's given me room to evaluate my priorities and to get more comfortable with *not* having a plan. There's a freedom in that, and I'm glad I've had a chance to experience it.

11.
A DOG WHISTLE
IN THE
MOUNTAINS

If you're going to do something this rash, you want to make it count. For me there was a sense, a pressure even, of needing to truly make a change—to do something entirely different but equally impressive because I had had the "dream job," so the chances of getting *another* one were slim to none (at least in my head). I also felt as if, hey, you quit so you could move forward, and if you don't do something completely different, you didn't really take advantage of the opportunity for change. And then surely other people would say, "Well, that was certainly much ado about not much."

I kept hoping that maybe I would fall out of love with the microphone. Or out of love with public radio. Each time I have a long stretch between fill-in gigs and I'm away from a studio for a while, I start to think I can do just fine without it. That becomes almost a relief, because it's very taxing to constantly be longing for something without knowing when you'll get it again. But then I get invited back in, and I have the time of my life, and the cycle starts all over again.

In early April 2014, I set aside two full weeks to work on this book. Dear friends offered their vacation home at Mammoth Mountain in California's eastern Sierra Nevada. The day I drove up, it was snowing, which is a treat for anyone who lives in the southern part of the state. Mammoth is flanked by Mount Whitney to the south, the highest point in the contiguous United States, and Yosemite to the north, one of the country's most treasured national parks. It is a spectacular place to get away with just your thoughts and a computer. I vowed to check e-mail only sporadically and focus on writing, writing, and writing some more. The only distraction was, well, everything outside the window.

I started each day with a four-mile walk around the village, just to clear my head. I found myself thinking about a different element of the book each morning. On day five, my thoughts turned to *Marketplace*, and the whole notion of leaving broadcasting altogether. I'd been struggling with how much of my departure story to share in this book. I started thinking about my audience, and how much I missed the microphone, and all of a sudden I just welled up with anger. I thought about the fact that the local public radio stations, while hiring me as a sub, didn't seem inclined in the slightest to take me off the market. I thought again about losing the NPR job. I started adding it all up, and the anger turned to tears. There I was, in this snowy paradise, with the sun shining, clean air filling my lungs at nine thousand feet, working on a book that someone was not just encouraging but actually paying me to research and write . . . and I was so, so angry. People would kill to be in my position, and I could hear their voices in my head accusing me of being an ungrateful lout. And at that moment I was one. While I was angry at all those other people and circumstances that led to my departure, I was also angry at myself. Why couldn't I just move on? Commit to the career change? Stop dabbling and start finding something else to do. Don't get angry ... get out. I cried behind my sunglasses for the last mile and a half of my walk. Here I was a year and a half after I'd left *Marketplace*, and I was still crying. Damn it! Cut. The. Cord.

By the time I got back to the cabin, I had resolved to move on, to embark on an in-depth search for a new career once I finished the book. It was as if I had cracked a bat over my own head and finally gotten with the program. I knew I would miss radio, but I also knew that I'd taken far too long to say my good-byes and get on with whatever was going to come next. The next part would be really hard, and that's probably why I had put it off for so long, but this walk felt like a catharsis. Yes, I needed to be done with my old self.

When I walked into the cabin, I washed the tears off my face, peeled off the layers of warm clothing, and checked my e-mail for the first time in a few days. It was about 10 a.m. There, in my inbox, sat a message from NPR. From the senior producer of the show I had done that big audition for, *All Things Considered*. He wrote to ask if there was any chance I was available to host that coming weekend. The guy who beat me out for the job was sick.

I'd like to be able to say that I took at least ten minutes to think about it. I mean, I had just been berating myself for going back over and over again to the lover who kept having me over for (really, *really* good) one-night stands but wouldn't commit. I had finally resolved to close the door behind me, once and for all, and I would set off in a new direction. I was all the way out in the woods, five hours from Los Angeles and NPR's Culver City studios, ensconced with all my research material and a few bottles of wine and a book deadline that was coming at me fast. This was no time to divert my attention.

"I am an author now, not a radio host, and I have a project that I need to complete, and I'm putting that whole broadcasting thing behind me anyway and moving on!" I said to myself. "If radio really loved me, it would've snatched me up when it had the chance. It was never meant to be, and I need to stop thinking that will change."

I wrote back to the producer, said I'd pack up and drive five hours back to LA, and that I'd see him the next morning.

III

The problem is that radio is like a dog whistle to me—it draws me back with a lure that I can't ignore. I can have long stretches when I am absolutely convinced that everything is going the way it's supposed to, that my life is taking a great new shape, and that I don't need radio anymore. As I said, the longer I go between hosting gigs, the less I miss it—at least that's what I've been telling myself.

But then I get behind the mic, and I'm hooked all over again. I have this itch to constantly be learning new things, talking with fascinating people, going places most people don't get to go, working in an exciting and fast environment, and knowing that I'm contributing to building a well-informed public. That last part sounds more than a little grandiose, but it's true. Journalists like having a hand in making other people more aware of the world they live in.

When I got back to Pasadena that night, after a long, spectacular blue-sky drive back down I-395 from the mountain, I started poring over the news coverage that I hadn't been paying any attention to in Mammoth. Ukraine, Russia, Syria, Boston Marathon bombing anniversary, Oscar Pistorius trial, Tax Day . . . I read up, then went to bed and set the alarm for my first day of work at NPR West in Culver City. I vividly remember smiling as I pulled up the covers and let a small laugh escape as I thought about the "crying walk" I'd taken that morning. The whole thing was crazycakes.

The next morning it took over an hour to go nineteen miles in LA traffic. I told myself this is what I would have had to endure every single day had I gotten the host position. I pulled up to the studios and chuckled at the parking spaces, which feature a small microphone painted on the cement. Microphones! My favorite thing!

I was concerned about how I would feel sitting in the chair I had so wanted to occupy. I worried that I'd be filled with regret and sadness for what-could-have-been. But instead, I was just utterly delighted to have this opportunity, even if only for the next five days. I walked in and one of the producers, whom I'd met during the audition process, gave me a big hug and welcomed me back to the show. The senior producer doled out a hug as well, and then it was time for the morning staff meeting.

I was so happy to be there. There's no loftier way to put it—I was just happy. I'd come to the meeting with some story and book interview suggestions, and a couple of them made it onto the show rundown. I got a refresher course in the system they use to write, edit, and produce stories. I found out I'd be interviewing musician and songwriter Aimee Mann later that week, as well as her new collaborator, rock musician Ted Leo. People love it when journalists interview famous people, so I made sure to post about it on social media, and the response was as enthusiastic as I'd expected.

For a weekend show, the workweek starts on Wednesday and goes through Sunday. You have Monday and Tuesday off. Wednesday is the first news meeting to talk about what you're going to cover, and the staff goes around the table pitching stories to the senior producer. Once the show producers and editors—and host—have decided on which stories to pursue, associate producers and interns start making calls and finding people to interview. That meant that the rest of my day was spent boning up on all the national and international news. Thursday I did a couple of interviews and more research and reading, and we started to firm up what story was going to appear on which show. The pace of those first couple of days wasn't too intense, but I had a lot of work to do, both at the office and when I got home in the evening.

Friday was bonkers. I did nine interviews that day alone. Nine conversations on several different topics, each one requiring an enormous amount of concentration to make sure it all sounded intelligent and comprehensible on air. I was completely spent by the end of the day, not just mentally but physically. I was exhausted. But I couldn't have been having any more fun. Yes, there was serious news to digest and explain, but just because it's serious, or even depressing, doesn't mean you can't love every minute of it. I was back in my element. I was immersed in journalism and in performance, and I had a microphone and producers, and I felt utterly fulfilled.

So much for moving on. I wondered if maybe what I'd really needed when I left *Marketplace* was a simple change of scenery, whether if in a different environment with the same work, I would have been just fine. That would certainly be an argument for getting a job before you quit. But in the landscape of my particular industry, the odds of getting a job comparable to what I had at *Marketplace* weren't good—those jobs are few and far between. And I didn't feel that I had the luxury of time to figure out what my other options might have been within the public broadcasting world. Was I hasty? Maybe. But I'd also lost some of the love I had for the job, and I had to leave it in order to get that love back. It's the whole absence-makes-the-heart-grow-fonder thing, as hackneyed as that might be.

And when you're popping in and out of temporary gigs, you're essentially immune to all the downsides that come with them. You're there, you do the job well, and you enjoy yourself, and then you leave. You're not dealing with the long-term vagaries of office politics, of an employer who does performance reviews, and of the stress that comes from doing something day in and day out, not just for a few days but for months and years on end. With job sampling, you just have the perks. That's not to say it's not hard work, because it almost always is, but you truly do not have to deal with the day-in-day-out BS that just about every full-time-job worker on the planet has to endure. So it's hard to compare the experiences, and that's a cautionary note to consider if you find yourself returning in some capacity to the job you've always done.

III

The push and pull of deciding whether to completely leave your former work life or keep part of it or go back to it altogether is made so much harder when you really love what you do. It's hard to imagine you'll find anything that can make you as happy and that will also satisfy things like . . . your bank account. My own story that week I returned to *Weekend All Things Considered* (WATC) reminded me of a coffee shop conversation I had with Sarah Sypniewski. I had met Sarah a few years before when I interviewed her for a radio story about the money we spend to care for our pets. She's big into animal rescue (as am I). She also coauthored, with her partner Kim Rogers, *Dog Photography for Dummies,* which features chapter titles like "Mutts and Bolts" and "Paws-ing for the Basics." Doggone it, they're hilarious!

Sarah wrote to me after I put out a call for career transition stories on Facebook. She hadn't read or seen my WDS speech, but she said she'd taken a leap of faith from her career a couple of years earlier and was willing to share. So we met up for coffee in LA's Silver Lake neighborhood.

Sarah's was a solidly middle-class upbringing. Her dad was a chemist. Her mom raised Sarah and three other kids, and she then worked in the corporate offices of Ace Hardware. They moved around a lot when Sarah was young, even though her dad's job wasn't in a traditionally upheaval-ridden industry. "Once I became an adult," she said, "I started realizing that he probably spent a lot of time looking for his own happiness in terms of a career." And that meant moving. In terms of defining success, "I don't think it was ever money based. I think it was more like how good we were as people."

Good grades were a given. So was college. And true to her parents' teachings, Sarah ended up going to grad school to study nonprofit leadership and management after completing an undergraduate degree in psychology. She did a stint with AmeriCorps, worked for the Red Cross for a while, and then began what she believed was a career and calling with the Los Angeles Gay and Lesbian Center, and its AIDS/LifeCycle event that features an annual fund-raising bike ride from San Francisco to LA. For six years she worked her way up the staff flowchart (getting fired and rehired along the way).

"I felt like I was successful in one major way, which was that I could pay my bills," she said. "I was finally out of debt. I was making a comfortable salary, ironically enough, in the nonprofit world. But I felt like I finally arrived."

It wasn't just the money though. Sarah felt like she was doing a lot of good. She was helping with a cause she held dear. And she adored her coworkers. It was fun, she told me, and they were all in it together.

It was a 24/7 lifestyle with a lot of pressure. The event was raising $13 million a year, but she said that it was never good enough for the people running the organization. Eventually the stress manifested itself in a lack of sleep, an elevated heart rate, and a loss of appetite. For six years, the job worked, and she was able to cope with the pressures. "And then, I decided that I wasn't happy. I didn't care, the money wasn't worth it, and I couldn't take it anymore." She felt pulled to leave. But she also loved the team she worked with. "Genuinely trusting people and being able to communicate honestly with somebody, it was a real treat. We had all seen a lot. That was one side of the internal debate about leaving. Then on the other side of the debate was my health."

As those words left her mouth, tears started to leave her eyes. And it had been three full years since her departure.

"I knew I would miss them. I didn't want to leave that experience. And I didn't want to leave a steady paycheck. I had no idea what I wanted to do. How will I formulate a plan? Very scary things. Of course, it was easier at the beginning, and then it got really hard for two years."

She left on her birthday. She didn't have another job lined up. She didn't have savings. She had three months of vacation that was paid out when she left and a supportive partner, Kim, who covered the rent when Sarah couldn't. She said her parents were scared for her, but proud, and friends said "go for it" and "good for you."

"At first I felt free. I felt like I could breathe. I felt like I could live like a normal human being. But it came crashing down probably around the four- or five-month mark."

What came crashing down was her personal economy. She wasn't making any money. It got so bad that she started eating only cereal because she didn't want to eat food bought with Kim's money. She was terrified and felt like an utter failure. "I would just be online all day oscillating between actively looking for jobs and trying to escape from my reality." She called herself a freelancer when friends asked what she was doing, but she was taking gigs that paid far below what she felt she was worth, and even those were few and far between. "There was a lot of tap dancing. I would turn the conversation and talk about what Kim was doing."

The hardest part, she said, aside from the money, was letting go of her passion for the work she'd done and for her coworkers. Even though she believed she'd done the right thing by leaving, the heartache persisted. So much so that three years later, talking about it made her choke up. Many people I know who have made the choice to leave a job they loved have had the same experience; it's so much harder to leave, and to move on, when you've truly found what you love doing and you are getting paid to do it. The emotional pull is significant, and it can leave a chasm in your psyche for a long time.

Since leaving, though, Sarah has written the book with Kim, and she has started her own business helping to find and rescue lost dogs throughout Los Angeles. (Her dog whistle was a literal one!) It took a while for the company, Ninjadog Concepts, to get traction, but it's growing, and she supplements that income with freelance writing, including greeting cards. And her definition of success has changed.

"I feel like I'm totally successful in terms of having conquered this status quo. I knew that I wasn't happy, and I did something to change it. I didn't have to settle. Of course, on the other hand, I'm still way below in terms of revenue and earnings. But I still earn enough to get by. I still feel like I'm sort of in this experiment. I don't feel like I have a career. I feel like I am bopping around a little bit."

The difference now is that she seems OK with that uncertainty, and with the change in circumstance. Sarah had to figure out what were the absolute necessities in her life, and what she could do without on the most basic, consumer levels. She moved the goalpost for herself and found a way to be happy, even though it meant a change in her lifestyle and a rethinking of what it means to have success. It's no longer about how well she's doing at her job. It's about how well she's doing lining up work for herself and the sense of accomplishment she gains from that process.

‖‖

Anita Agarwal graduated with a double major from Barnard College, got an entry-level consulting job with a large multinational company, got laid off, worked with an international development program in India, went back to school for her MBA at Emory, and promptly got another consulting job, a six-figure salary, and was on track to make partner.

"You just kind of keep staying and staying," she said, "and even when I was in it, I had my ups and downs, but initially I was really trying hard to be the consultant personality, which is very outgoing and sales-y and sort of fast talking. I was just exhausted doing that, and I felt like I kept getting all this feedback on how I needed to improve this and improve that. And finally I just said, 'Screw it, if they want to fire me, they can; I'm just going to be myself.' And that's when I actually started doing a lot better. I started getting promoted, and I started getting raises. I started getting really good roles, and I started working on different projects. I actually learned a lot, even while I was there. For instance, they'd make us go to recruiting events to hire new people. And I actually had really good things to say about the company. I would say, 'Yeah, it's exhausting, and it's stressful, but you learn a lot.'"

The problem, she said, was that the industry had what she called an "up-or-out" model. Successful employees were expected to continue rising through the ranks, whether they wanted to or not. I have a close family member who is in a similar line of work, where the only way to gain more money, even respect, is to take on higher-ranking positions, even if it's not a job you want. There seem to be few rewards in the American workplace for simply doing your job well and consistently, for keeping the engines humming along. I'm not saying that rewards should automatically come just because you're doing your job, but the pressure to keep climbing the ladder seems misplaced. And for Anita, that pressure became too much to bear. Less than ten years into her career, she jumped.

"In consulting, it's kind of like a pyramid. You enter at the bottom, and then basically the way they keep you performing at a high level, and the way they keep the best of the best, is that you're always getting promoted. Basically, after three or four years, you have to move up to the next level or you get asked to leave."

She didn't want to make partner. She didn't want to take on the responsibilities, tasks, and lifestyle that went with that level of the company. It was too much, and it was not the life she wanted for herself. Less than a decade into her career, she was burned out and needed a break.

"I knew I was doing everything that a successful person is supposed to do," she wrote in an e-mail to me. "But all the money and brand names were no longer buying me happiness. For a time I started purchasing expensive handbags because I could, and I thought that was what I was supposed to do as a successful person. But a voice inside me was telling me that none of these things would address the deep dissatisfaction that I felt."

She ran into someone at a wedding who had quit her job in advertising without a plan, taken five months off, and had no trouble finding a new job afterward. Anita went to work the following Monday, asked for a six-month leave of absence, and went off on a solo trip around the world—visiting Mexico, Spain, Thailand, Indonesia, the Philippines, and Japan. When she got home, she promptly resigned without a plan in sight.

She moved back in with her parents and freelanced for a while. She started a jewelry sales business with a friend, but eventually she abandoned that business because it wasn't fulfilling. "I wasn't having fun with it anymore," she told me later. "I just felt like the whole point of leaving my job and doing all this stuff was to have fun with whatever I did next." But at the same time, she felt like a total failure because she'd walked away from a second career. She was embarrassed to tell people. "I didn't really know what it was like to fail, after going to top schools and then getting brand-name jobs. I felt like . . . the universe had told me that I was never meant to do these wild and crazy things I had dreamed up. But finally I had to come out and embrace the failed venture and my feelings toward it."

She was running out of money, and she wanted to move out of her parents' house. So Anita decided her best option was to go back to what she knew. Not because she loved it but out of necessity.

"With a heavy heart, I applied to corporate jobs, and I just started a new one. I'm glad to have a paycheck and health insurance again. But the last two years were filled with a lot of personal development and creativity, which has been amazing. I already have a mental timeline of when I will be leaving this job to head out to greener pastures. There's this Indigo Girls song called 'Closer to Fine' in which they talk about going from point A to point B, and it's not always a straight line. It's crooked. And I realize that the song totally applies to me. I get it now. I felt like I was following a very strict path, and then finally I realized there is no straight line. And that's OK."

III

Katherine Sullivan (a pseudonym) was forty-two when we first chatted in the fall of 2013. Like Sarah, Katherine was born in Illinois, but she had lived most of her adult life in the Bay Area, and she is now in Portland, Oregon. Her dad worked in computer programming and development, including an astronomy project for NASA, and her mom was a librarian in an anthropology museum. "I guess the message I always got was 'Be educated, be smart, and hang out with smart, interesting people. We don't really care what your career is, but follow what's really interesting,'" Katherine told me. In her house, it was never about money but about achieving some sort of educational status. She majored in classics at a top UC school and had started on a track toward a PhD, but then she dropped out after two months and ended up becoming a corporate attorney. The law degree, Katherine said, was the quickest way to have safety. Just get the degree, get a top law firm job, make a ton of money, and pay off the school loans. "And at some point there, I kind of lost myself."

She began practicing corporate transaction law in 2002, at the height of the corporate scandals that brought down Enron, WorldCom, Adelphia, Arthur Andersen, and more. A few years later she found herself practicing investment management law just as the 2008 global financial crisis reared its head. Katherine was starting to feel a cognitive dissonance between what she believed in and what she was doing.

"I felt outwardly successful. I had a job at an elite world-class law firm. I was making a lot of money. I had nice clothes that I wore to work, but I would get home and put on my jeans and hiking clothes. The fancy restaurants got old after a while, so I would just go because I had to. I would get these fat paychecks, and I was just socking away money and paying down my loans."

She practiced corporate law for eight years. In 2008, the financial company she was working for as in-house counsel was sold to another giant firm, and she felt increasingly out of place. "I took a week off and rented a little cabin in a small bucolic town in Northern California, and I was just there by myself for a week. And I realized if I didn't stop this train, I was going to be really stuck."

At that time, she was thirty-nine years old, with a milestone birthday on the way. She was about to buy a house. She didn't know what she wanted to do next. She felt physically ill thinking about getting off the track that she'd set out for herself. She had nightmares.

When she got back from the week away, she knew she had to pull the trigger immediately or she'd change her mind. She called her real estate broker to cancel the purchase the Sunday she returned, and on Monday morning she went into her boss's office and quit. He wanted to know what other firm she was leaving for, and she replied that she was taking a year off to travel and didn't know what would come after that. He tried to get her to stay as long as possible, but she said she was done. "After I had a conversation with him, I had a conversation with his boss, and then his boss, and each level was more convinced that I was crazy."

Katherine knows she's fortunate in that she had money saved up from a lucrative job, and she had no mortgage or kids or spouse to enter the quitting equation. But that doesn't mean it was easier for her than for the rest of us. I asked whether she had ever asked herself, "What the hell did I do?"

"Oh, my gosh, every day. Every day that I woke up after I gave notice I was scared. And then when I was traveling, I was scared. What the hell am I going to do when I get back? Actually, I don't say 'hell.' I say the F word. I tried to meditate after going to a meditation retreat in Italy. But the whole year I was thinking, 'What am I going to do when I get back?' But when I came back, I still didn't know what to do. I still don't know what to do."

In the meantime, she moved to Portland and started a coaching and consulting practice, working with executives who wanted to improve their interpersonal skills. (I could have sent a whole passel of clients her way had I known.) She enjoyed it, but she found that she wasn't a good fit for running her own business. Before, she had traded her freedom and values for financial security. Now, she'd given up the financial security for freedom, and certainly enjoyed that part, but she discovered she didn't have the skills or capacity to be entrepreneurial. "I don't have that gene," she admitted. "I want a structure to fit into. I want colleagues. Memory can be deceptive, but I even have fond memories of cubical life."

That seems to be a common experience. Once you're out of the situation that drove you crazy or made you sad, you start focusing on all of the good things that you loved about that place, whether it was colleagues or location or clients, or even the coffee. You wonder why you left, and you wonder if you should have stuck it out, if really, things weren't *that* bad. But as Katherine said, memory can be deceptive. In reality, they probably were that bad.

For her, the idea of returning to a structure, and colleagues, was a dog whistle to take the bar exam in Oregon. She did, and she passed. She told me that she wanted to tease out threads, to figure out "What am I missing." Taking the exam also meant she would have a law license as an option. She had done a con-tracted law project that she loved, so she was trying to figure out what exactly excited her about it. Was it the intellectual challenge? The energy of the environment? Problem solving? She thought maybe she could have a solo law practice. But then shortly after the exam, she had what she called a massive, soul-crushing dark spell because she realized didn't want to be self-employed anymore, in any business.

"What I really missed was feeling competent—not that I wasn't feeling competent with coaching clients, but I was feel-ing completely incapable as a business owner. I missed feeling busy. . . . I realized I missed being in a thriving organization where stuff needed to get done all the time. And I reached the point where I realized there was BS everywhere, and I was just going to have to make some compromises. I did miss the law, I missed things about it—I guess what I've been trying to figure out is how much of that is unique to the practice of law."

That's the echo of a dog whistle. I'm sure of it. And Kath-erine's experience mirrors mine in so many ways. We both have sampled from buffets, trying different things to test out what works (what tastes good!) and what doesn't. Professor Herminia Ibarra, when writing about career identities, says it's important to explore our "many possible selves": "We learn who we have become—in practice, not in theory—by testing fantasy and reality, not by 'looking inside.'" Test every variable individually to see how you react to each one in your life and try to keep emotion out of it. Easier said than done, as always, but worth the effort.

I saw on social media, several months after our last conver-sation, that Katherine was hanging out a shingle. She opened her own law firm. It had been a journey of more than two years for her, and she expressed some fear and trepidation about striking out on her own in the profession in which she once had an enormous support structure to cushion any blows. But her excitement was palpable. And so was her well-deserved pride.

III

I tried putting myself "on the couch" a couple of times over those few days I was at NPR. I wanted to understand how this all played into the ongoing push and pull of uncertainty that comes with figuring out what to do next after you leave a career. For five glorious days, I was "NPR's Tess Vigeland." Even though I was only there to keep a chair warm, it made me feel as if I had returned home after a really long trip. And as any regular traveler knows, even a few days of home can be enough to give comfort that you still belong there.

For all of that, though, I didn't have the what-if moments I thought I might. I enjoyed every minute in the newsroom and in the studio, but I didn't let myself go down the path of oh-maybe-they'll-bring-me-back-again or oh-maybe-this-or-that—I left that to friends and family who were sure that's what all this fill-in work was leading to. And that was a psychological shift for me. I relished those five days, and when they were over, I told myself to remember what the past year and a half had taught me, which is to be open to what might come along and to not obsess about the future so much.

The week with WATC felt like a microcosm of what I'd learned and experienced since leaving *Marketplace*. The roller coaster was clearly still going, and I still had a lot of emotions to sort through. But my reaction to all of it was more thoughtful, and more restrained, than I think it would have been a year earlier, when I would have been asking "What does this *mean*? Will I be the main backup now? Maybe someone at NPR headquarters heard me and will offer me a job!"

No, instead, I left the studio with no expectations that I would host the show again—although I did, four more times, over the course of the year. And because I had that mindset, if they did ask me back, it would just be more gravy (or frosting, or whatever your chosen metaphor of deliciousness). It's not an easy mindset to keep, and I did struggle with it each time I went back. But I think a few things were going on. First, as I've described before, not getting that host job was the biggest blow of my professional career, but the fact that they asked me back, even as a fill-in, helped to soften that blow over time, and that gave me more confidence in the future. Second, though it took me a long time to accept this, I've realized it doesn't have to be an either-or proposition. I don't have to either be *in* radio or *out*. This was a tough mental struggle, and I think only time made it possible for me to say, "Hey, I'm glad to keep my hands in it, and sure, maybe someday I'll go back for good, but for now, at least I have a few days and weeks here and there, and people still want me on their air." And third, if nothing else, going back again and again to my first love showed me how important it is to my own personal satisfaction. Even if I only get a little bit here and there, at least I get that taste, which is more than most people can say.

All in all, I feel like this part of the process was yet more proof that, within the leap, you don't have to conduct your career, or your life for that matter, the way everybody else does it, or the way you always expected to. Screw the rules. Pretend there aren't any and see what happens.

I sometimes still hope that I'll fall out of love with the microphone, with my career. But, mostly, I tell myself that there's no reason to tune out the dog whistle.

12.
REDEFINING SUCCESS AND WORK

Several years ago, I interviewed the noted author and Big-Thinker Alain de Botton about a book he'd just written called *The Pleasures and Sorrows of Work.* It was the first year of the Great Recession—2009—and people were losing jobs at a rate that was difficult for most of us to wrap our heads around. He came on the air to talk about what work means to us, what its purpose is, and the upsides and downsides of work. In the interview, I commented that those were also the questions we ask about life in general, so I wondered what that said about how much our work has *become* our lives.

"Well, it's true that for most of recorded human history, work was something that people did," he answered, "but it wasn't where they expected to put their center of meaning and their hope for a good life. But ever since about the middle of the eighteenth century, in the United Kingdom and the United States, we've moved toward a different system that really identifies work with the meaning of life. So you work for money, sure, but you work for deeper reasons: for identity, for self-fulfillment, for growth. Not having a job, not being in employment, is kind of a shameful condition. Because you're not only lacking any money but also an identity."

The Great Recession at the end of the first decade of the new century changed the notion of unemployment being a shameful condition. Job loss became so prevalent that it also became unsurprising, and because of that, it lost a lot of the stigma that's usually associated with it. That didn't mean that people who experienced it felt any better about it, but the sense of profound shame that often accompanied being fired or laid off seemed a tiny bit diminished just because it had become such a common thing. We heard as much on the show from callers who told us what a relief it was every time we talked to someone else who had lost a job. So many others throughout the country were experiencing the same self-doubt, fear, mental and emotional anguish, and I think hearing that was a salve for the intense hurt and sense of betrayal-writ-large that always accompanies a job loss. Misery loves company because it makes you feel less alone, awkward, and ashamed. We tried, week in and week out, to tell people that they shouldn't feel as if they'd lost their identity just because they'd lost their job. They weren't deemed unsuccessful now just because of someone else's bottom-line decision. When we would interview people who had decided to go down a path less ordinary as a next step after a layoff (including two people who had started their own cheesemaking businesses!), we always heard from listeners who thanked us for reminding them that there were other options worth exploring.

I also tried to talk a lot about the new landscape of the

workforce, where people were reinventing themselves as entrepreneurs or super-small business owners every day. Startups and self-employment situations are so much more common than they used to be. While job security is harder and harder to come by these days, job potential is more varied than ever before. We've entered the era of making a profit off of your personal brand, with websites such as Etsy, and a culture that makes it possible to succeed just by being an Internet celebrity of some sort. So if you have a funny-looking (grumpy?) cat, by all means snap a photo, put it on Instagram, and see what happens! The traditional job market has failed so many people, but the one upside is that the economy supports all manner of new enterprises, and that makes it less and less "shameful" to not have traditional employment. I put quotes around that word because I don't think it should be at all shameful in the first place—employment is never guaranteed, and the only feeling we should have for people facing unemployment is deep compassion and a desire to help.

What a job loss forces you to do—whether you leave on your own accord or whether you get laid off or fired—is take a long, hard look at what makes you unique. You have to ask yourself what makes you remarkable, not as a working being but as a human being. If this leap taught me anything, it's that I needed to recalibrate my notions of what makes me important, what makes me valuable, and what role work plays in both of those things.

Finding a new definition of success is probably the biggest challenge of all in this process. Everyone I talked with about this experience, even the people who took a leap of their own volition, said they'd been forced to confront what success now meant to them, because they could no longer fit into the traditional definitions that included money, title, office, upward trajectories, and beyond. Our definitions are outward facing, and they owe so much to our working lives rather than our inward sense of self. For almost everyone I interviewed, figuring out what made them successful in the middle of or after a leap required figuring out what success meant outside of work.

For Margie Weinstein, the experience started with wanting to redefine not just success but what purpose her work served. Margie is a member of that North Stars group of women in New York that gets together every month or so to talk about their own leaps from their careers and help each other through the process of finding the next one.

"I feel like I have these things that were real," she told me, "and that created this sense of accomplishment, but now when I ask myself, 'What is success? Am I successful?' it gnaws at me less. Mostly I'm wanting to feel challenged and wanting to feel like my life is meaningful, more than successful. I think that in part prompted my decision to want to leave the museum world. I do fundamentally believe that art matters, but I wanted to do something that was more in direct service. I worry less about whether I will ever find something as great as my other job or that is the next upward step. I genuinely am using different metrics."

Those metrics are admittedly squishy, but they fit into a larger pattern of what so many American workers say they want from their careers now. Arianna Huffington tapped into this with her bestselling self-help book *Thrive*, which argues that "wellness" is just as important, if not more important, than power and money in defining success. Of course,

I'd parry that it's much easier to define success as wellness, rather than money or power, when you already have a whole lot of money and power. But that old chestnut about how you'll never say on your deathbed you wish you'd worked more is true no matter what you have in your bank account.

For Margie, the new definition revolved around finding a way to make a difference in the political arena, which wasn't necessarily remunerative or glamorous but that gave her a broader meaning and purpose. "So many studies have shown that we all want to feel like we're contributing to something larger than ourselves. And that is really important to me. You know [the author] Po Bronson makes the distinction between being happy—that is, finding happiness in work—and finding meaning in work. And that made sense to me. I was really happy in my other job, and I did find it meaningful. But right now, I think in this second phase of my career, I would never say that I didn't want to be happy, but I feel like if I find something meaningful, I'll derive a lot of satisfaction from that rather than just simply being happy. So I think those are the things that gnaw at me way more than the conventional notions of success."

Wendy Harris, one of the other North Stars, said she was still working hard to stop introducing herself as a lawyer, because it had defined her for so long. "I'm so much more than that," she told me. "It's hard to step off the path of what is considered successful because we're constantly told that that's what we should want. But I think what it really is, is that there's this utter fear of failure. And honestly [no matter what anybody else thinks], my mom thinks I'm going to be fine. My dad's proud of me for walking away from the 'successful' job to do this other thing. And as long as I have that, I feel pretty good."

Aaron McHugh, who went through his daughter's unimaginable medical challenge, realized that he needed to find another way to define his life, and the work within it. The definition of success became an internal barometer instead of an external one. He said he spent a lot of time looking for others, whether it was coworkers or industry peers, to validate his efforts and ideas.

"I would kind of always keep one eye on the bleachers to see what the feedback was. What I've done now is to say, I'm going to do my best work to the best of my ability the best way I know how, and some people may not like it, and that's OK. I'd rather lose or not be successful in my job or not be a fit for a company or whatever, but leave it all on the field the way I know to leave it instead of always wrestling and feeling concerned about 'What if I don't do it right? What if the applause meter isn't high enough?' And the irony of this is that now I'm less committed to what job I have and more committed to how I want to work and the kind of company I want to work for. I'm really able to lead, instead of always feeling like my success is subject to other people's applause meter." And so far, he says, it's working.

I relate to that notion of constantly concerning yourself with the applause meter. Of course in broadcasting, I lived with a sort-of applause meter my entire career. Only it's called a People Meter, and it's run by a company called Arbitron that tells you whether anyone is listening to your show. I tried not to worry about those numbers too much when they came out twice a year (these days broadcasters get numbers much more frequently), but it was an external indication of whether the listening public liked the job I was doing. I augmented that literal meter with the comments I'd get at public appearances and in letters and tweets and other feedback that listeners chose to give. I loved having strangers say, "Oh! I know that show! Love it and love you!" when they heard my name or my voice. All of those responses contributed to my applause meter—as did annual reviews and whatever feedback I got from my employers over the years.

There's nothing wrong with any of this except when it becomes the *only* way you place a value on yourself. Dorie Clark, author of *Reinventing You: Define Your Brand, Imagine Your Future*, told me it's natural to seek out the approval of others, but you shouldn't let it define you. "We're constantly, as humans, looking for external validation," she said. "It's the social proof concept in psychology. If we're meeting people for the first time and we're trying to tell if they're legitimate or not, we look at, well, what college did they go to, what companies did they work for, whom are they affiliated with, and so on. And if other people have judged them to be worthy, then we can relax our guard and say, OK, they're probably legitimate. Similarly, unless you have a very strong internal compass, it's hard to feel good about having a meandering path that leads you through the wilderness at times. You get worried because you can't tell if you're cutting through the forest on the way to something great or if you're lost in the woods. So we're looking for social proof in our own lives. Oh, well, if I have job with a prominent company, then I must be OK. And that can really lull you into a kind of complacency." A complacency that can keep you in a job that's no longer the right fit.

I still crave external signs, and some of my happiest moments over the past couple of years have been when I announce that I'm going to be back on the airwaves, and I get all kinds of virtual high-fives and excitement from those who are following me along on this experiment. I also know that there is still a cool factor in what I used to do, and what I do every so often now, and I won't pretend that it's no big deal when people respond to that. Lady Gaga sings that she lives "for the applause, applause, applause," and I can't blame her for doing so. But now that I've created a little more of a separation between myself and that external applause meter, I realize that I can glean enormous satisfaction and pride by doing things for myself. I now take delight in small victories that I might not have even registered before. For example, I was putting together some voiceover work, and I realized at one point I'd said "forty-seven years old" when it was supposed to be "ninety-seven years old." I didn't want to book more studio time, so I went back through the copy to see if I had said "ninety-seven" anywhere else, I found audio where I had done exactly that, and I was able to make a seamless computer edit to correct the mistake. It's such a teeny, teeny, tiny thing, but I was so delighted with my own *genius* and the editing skill I'd acquired over a twenty-year career in audio, that it made my day. You don't realize until you're away from your job just how many skills you have that others don't. You don't realize it when you're in a workplace because you're surrounded by other people who do the same thing. But after being away from it, those small victories become part of the success metrics you can set for yourself. These days, I try to make a mental note of those victories, if not a tally. Maybe it's time to set up a tally and give myself a performance review based on that? Note to self.

Nat Katz, the Episcopal-priest-in-training, told me about the mental shifts that have helped him redefine what success means, and particularly what it means in his career. "I've ceased to use the term 'career,'" he said. "I talk about 'vocation' instead. I think 'career' assumes a linear path; it assumes you are both fit for and will be satisfied by one thing over the course of your life. We use the term 'vocation' because it's not linear. It makes it more values based." And if we turn from the Good Book to *Webster's*, Nat is right—a *vocation* is a "strong feeling of suitability for a particular career or occupation." It's easy to see how a "feeling" is much more fluid than a career. If you're focused on the feeling—satisfaction, challenge, enrichment, whatever else it is that you're looking for—then it becomes less about the act that gives you that feeling. Suddenly, what matters has much less to do with the external applause meter and much more to do with the internal validation. If you think of what you do as a vocation, it certainly seems like first, you would make sure it's suitable for you, and second, it would be easier to wrap your head around change.

When Nat marked that mental line for me—between a career and a vocation—I tried to think of my own twenty years in broadcasting as a vocation to see if the definition fit. Fortunately for me, it did. I had a *very* strong feeling of suitability for my occupation. But the word *vocation* really breaks down that idea of the "sunk-cost" argument from earlier, where you feel like you're wasting years of already-invested time and effort. Maybe you just lost that feeling for a while, or forever, and you're meant to find something else that's equally suitable. It's a mental mind game that's worth trying out. If we all have vocations, then there is almost an underlying assumption that change will come eventually—we can feel called to do one thing, then another, then another. The investment builds upon itself, and that is much easier to justify psychologically, assuming you have that mental hurdle to clear.

Nat also noted that the ideas about vocation that have been passed down from (Biblical) time immemorial, whether in work or in any other area of your life, are building blocks to becoming a fuller person.

"In the Christian tradition we express in this notion of pilgrimage, that there are long journeys. This is a human paradigm, that there are times in life that call us out of our comfort zones—sometimes by our choice, sometimes not by our choice—that this is part of the human experience. That's where the season of Lent comes from. Into the desert for forty days, and it's this time of fasting and trial and penitence but also mindfulness, of letting go. This is how I applied it to my situation. You go on a journey through the desert, and you bring only what you have to. Along the way, through what feels like isolation, what feels like alienation, what feels like being separated, you actually discover what is real and what is not. This is not just part of life. It is part of the tradition of people who have gone before me, who experienced this in all different kinds of ways, and they've thought about it in this context, and they've come out the other side of it with a feeling that they are closer to God, more at peace with themselves, and have a greater sense of self-knowledge, and a deeper ability to connect with other people as a result."

The hard choices, he added, are the ones that are the richest. There's something to be learned and taken away.

"You can look back on your life and say, 'Gee, maybe I made the wrong decision,' but there's so much to be gained in life from the act of choosing. There's plenty of opportunities not to. But the act of choosing faithfully is not ever something that's to be regretted."

And that's another way I'm trying to measure my own success—whether I can, ultimately, truly believe that when I leaped from my career, I did the right thing and that whether it worked out perfectly or not (not!), I don't regret it. I'm slowly getting to that point, and slowly believing that, as everyone said to me right after I quit, I am brave. Some days I feel righteous in that decision; some days I still feel like a fool, especially every time I'm back behind the microphone (that darn dog whistle). Every time I leave a fill-in radio gig—*every time*—I have major pangs of regret. They're so significant that I have told some of the people in charge at those places that I just need to make a clean break without the emotional turmoil (that stems from having such a fun time, go figure). Then I change my mind, because avoiding those opportunities would be robbing myself of the chance to do what I love and what I do best. Who does that to themselves? The fact that I still feel like this about my chosen ... vocation! ... tells me I'm right not to abandon it wholesale, at least not right now. It tells me that I made the right choice, because my love for it has gotten stronger instead of weaker. Clearly, I needed some kind of break.

The reality of trying to redefine success is that none of us live in a bubble. Reality intrudes, as do societal expectations, and as Carl Seidman noted in one of our long conversations, those expectations and definitions are hard to fend off, even if you've gone a long way toward finding those new definitions.

"I don't want to lose the sense of realism that I have now,

and almost the degree of spirituality, where I feel like I'm just at peace in the world, and that's OK. You don't have to do something remarkable. You don't have to be constantly grow- ing and proving yourself. You have to get comfortable and not feel the external pressure of society's saying, 'You need to do this; you need to do that.' You have to be OK with whatever standards you set for yourself."

And that is an enormous challenge, no matter what your chosen work. I won't pretend it's easy. Without all those exter- nal mechanisms to show whether I'm successful or not, I've had to come up with new, internal definitions. Do I like the project I'm working on? Am I satisfied with how I'm managing my time? How much do I find myself missing what I used to do, and can I somehow make up for that feeling by going after something else? Am I doing enough to generate work, or am I leaving too much to the fates and serendipity? And, yes, am I happy? Am I getting an emotional and psychological lift from the work I do have? All of those questions have factored in to my new notions of success. Getting to the point where you don't care what other people think? It's a very faraway point from where most of us live. I know for sure that I'm not there yet. I'm not sure I'll ever get there. But I feel healthier for try- ing. I feel as if I'm getting better at appreciating my own sense of accomplishment, whether anyone else notices or not.

13.
GETTING BACK TO REMARKABLE

There's a popular quote that talks about a moment when you have to decide between turning the page or closing the book. I think I turned the page on radio, but I haven't yet closed the book. Every once in a while I still wonder if taking my leap was the biggest mistake of my life. I wonder if I should never have gone into my boss's office with that white envelope back in 2012, even though leaving has brought me all kinds of other opportunities for which I'm beyond grateful. It's an emotional turmoil that isn't over yet, even after putting the book project together, writing down the experience of leaping without a net, of sewing my parachute on the way down. And you know what? It would be so much easier to go back to what I used to do—assuming someone would want me to do so. Just give me a microphone and a studio. I'm really good at it and . . . I loved it. Thoreau said to never look back unless you're planning to go that way. Right now, on many days, that way seems like it would be comforting.

But if I hadn't left, I would never have spent the time figuring out who I am outside of what I do. I wouldn't have reevaluated my priorities for what I want my life to look like. I wouldn't have realized how my skills could serve me, and others, in new and different ways—heck, I wouldn't have realized just how many skills I have. One of the things I noticed along the way was that I actually got better at my old job, on the occasions I went back to it, because I was fearless. I wasn't trying to impress anyone anymore. I was no longer comparing myself to other people in my old newsroom, and that freedom actually made me more comfortable on air, more willing to take risks and be myself. Basically, I'm having more fun, and based on the response from colleagues and the audience, that translates into great radio. I thought I was good already, but the leap has made me even better. So why look back? It's taken time, but I finally feel like I'm moving *toward* something instead of leaving something behind.

One quote from my WDS speech that I hear about people latching on to again and again is this:

"I do think it is wise though, throughout your working life, to take time to reevaluate what you're doing, what you really love about it, and what you don't. Because I didn't do that very much. And I should have, *even* though I thought I was in my dream job. Dream while you're in the dream."

I want to reiterate that now. You don't know what might happen down the line in your career. Even if you love it now, you might not love it next year. Even if you feel safe in your position now, you might not feel so safe in six months. Industries change in a heartbeat, and as we all know so well at this point, the economy operates on a knife's edge. You never know what's happening beneath the surface. Good times can turn ugly *very quickly*. So start thinking about some of these larger questions while you're comfortable, so that you don't have to start from scratch at a point that is uncomfortable.

I'm not saying you have to have a plan B. I am saying that if your life, and your self-identity, revolves around your work, and you clamor to get to the top, it's worth considering who you will be if all that goes away, either voluntarily or involuntarily. I want you to do what I didn't do, which is to contemplate some of these questions before you ever face them head on. What would your absolutely worst-case scenario look like? Do you have a supportive partner or circle of family and friends who can function as a sounding board, without discouraging you from doing what's *best* for you, instead of what's *expected* of you? Have you thought about what it is that drives you in your career? What's your motivation? Is that the right motivation? If not, what would be?

Earlier I cited the work of Herminia Ibarra, author of *Working Identity: Unconventional Strategies for Reinventing Your Career*. I talked about her three-part definition of *career change*, including (1) experimenting with side projects and (2) tweaking your network to reflect careers you might want to explore. Did you notice I didn't tell you the third part? I wanted to save it for this chapter, because that third element is that you *must* have a story to tell. I've told mine in these pages. If you are leaping, or want to, you need to figure out what your story is. "You must be able to explain yourself to other people," Herminia told me, "because on the face of it, this kind of change often makes no sense. So if *you* don't make sense of it, it's very hard to get *others* to help you. Know how to tell your life story and why this is happening. What is it that is causing you to make such a big and radical change?"

I think that's the best advice you could possibly take away. If you can figure out how to tell your story with grace and humor, if you can force yourself to answer those questions, you'll save yourself a lot of grief in your leap. You'll be prepared for those questions at the dinner party, you'll already have a sense of what kind of metrics of success work for you, and you'll trust yourself more because you will have already gone through the mental exercise of figuring out your own motivations. Oh, how I wish I'd done all that! But, hey, at least now I have a book's worth of it.

I I I

I'm sure some of you came to this book for the answers on "how to do it"—how to quit your job without having a plan B. I get it. And I could have written that book: *Ten Steps to Quitting Your Job and Finding Your Passion.* But I didn't write that book because I can't tell you how to do that. Nobody can. Jodi Ettenberg, a travel writer and blogger who quit her job as an attorney to travel the world when she was in her late twenties, tells people who visit her site legalnomads.com for The Answers that "your mileage will vary." In other words, your experience will not mirror mine. She doesn't want to tell people—her fans, her readers—how to live or how to do anything, for that matter. "A lot of my energy is focused on reframing people's expectations of me," she told me, "because people so desperately want someone to tell them how to do it. I'm going to tell you the things that helped me along the way, but I'm not an expert in what you think I am. I'm just trying to do something in life that I'm excited about, but that also teaches me as much as possible every day." Ditto.

It's not as simple as following someone else's model for how to get off the beaten path. What I hope I've done here is give you a sense of what it's like to leap and what you can expect from the experience. Although everyone's journey is different, I hope that you can take some comfort in the fact that lots of other people are struggling with it just as you are and that it's not as easy as following your passion and making it happen. All that said, the stories in this book show that it *is* possible. You should plan financially—certainly more than I did—and you should prepare psychologically for a process that will take time. Do the soul-searching, ask hard questions, and don't be afraid of whatever answers come back. Your mileage will vary, and that's OK.

III

There's a phrase that you will likely hear a lot after you've taken your leap that I started to loathe over the last couple of years: "I can't wait to see what you do next!"

I know it's well meaning, and I appreciate the sentiment. But, and maybe this is just me, I have always felt like that phrase was loaded with expectation. What if what I do next is boring? What if it's completely pedestrian, and it has nothing to do with journalism or the radio or even a microphone? What if I'm your new meter maid, or delivery girl, or your customer service representative (all jobs that are necessary and that I have total respect for)? You *can* wait to see *that*, right?

When people said or wrote that to me, the voice inside my head filled in the rest of the thought bubble like this: "I can't wait to see what you do next ... because it will be awesome and enviable just like the rest of your career has been!" President George W. Bush talked about "the soft bigotry of low expectations." But what I felt was the hard weight of high expectations—expectations that I might not meet.

And I still am not sure that I will.

This book was a yearlong reprieve from having to figure out what I want to do when I grow up. Now I'm wondering if maybe I should, indeed, get a copy of *What Color Is Your Parachute?* because I *still* don't know what's next. Maybe I have to go out and network (ugh) and hustle (ugh ugh) and tweet and Link-In (ugh ugh ugh) just like every other job hunter. Maybe I have to say yes to stuff I want to say no to. Maybe I should go back to what I know, or maybe I should leave journalism for good. All those questions from my time up at Mammoth—they're still there. It's embarrassing. Surely, an adult with more than two decades of work experience can figure out for herself what she wants to do. Especially when she has so much time to think about it and explore her options. I'm smart, I'm capable, and it's up to me to get my ass in gear and come up with some answers instead of just asking these questions over and over again.

But the struggle is constant, and I cannot wrap this up in a neat little bow. It ends in uncertainty. And the best that I've been able to do is to get more comfortable being uncomfortable, to accept the uncertainty and not let it dominate my attention. It's still not easy. I still wonder what's coming. I still worry that I've already had the best job I will ever have and that nothing I do from here on out will measure up to what I've already accomplished. I still worry about a steady paycheck, and I still worry about how I'll feel if I don't top myself in whatever comes after all this.

But another part of me is proud of this new world order I've established for myself. I was *brave*. My world didn't fall apart when I stepped off the ladder I'd been climbing my entire life. I'm still remarkable in ways I didn't even know before my leap. My definition of success is changing, and I think it's a healthier one that doesn't rely on title or money or fame. I'm still evolving into that definition. Focusing on externalities like money and prestige is a hard habit to break.

But it's possible, and if you take nothing else away from this book, I want you to start breaking those habits and figuring out what you really, honestly need from your career. What's the balance of paycheck, challenge, energy, and everything else that you need in order to be the most fulfilled and, yes, the most happy? It's hard work to come up with that balance, which is why so many of us never bother to ask ourselves the question. And we're busy enough with all the detritus of daily life that delving into some of this stuff just seems extraneous and, well, there's always tomorrow to think about. And you know what? Sometimes gratitude can be what's holding you back. If you have a career you've loved, if you've gathered a decent paycheck, if you've been able to support a family and put a roof over your head and go out for dinner and drinks every once in a while, it's easy to tell yourself that you should just be grateful for what you have, and good enough is good enough. And sometimes it is! But if you have a yearning, if you have that thing going on with the bad deck of cards and you just know something isn't right, if you find yourself asking what it would be like to just chuck it all and start over ... if you have any of those thoughts, it's beyond time to start asking some really tough questions of yourself and exploring your options. To paraphrase Lao Tzu, the father of Taoism, you—and I—will have to truly let go of who we are in order to become what we might be. I've come a long way on that front, but I still have work to do.

The week I left *Marketplace*, one of my closest friends gave me a refrigerator magnet that I still keep on the wall in my office at home. It says LEAP AND THE NET WILL APPEAR. I didn't believe it at the time, as much as I loved and appreciated her gesture. But I believe it now. I've had several nets appear since then, some real, some metaphorical. Some of them held me, some of them bounced me back up in the air. But I'm grateful and fortunate for every one of them.

I'm confident they will appear for you too.

And I can't wait to see what you do next.

NOTES

1. Signing Off

1. http://www.forbes.com/sites/jeannemeister/2012/08/14/job
   -hopping-is-the-new-normal-for-millennials-three-ways-to-prevent
   -a-human-resource-nightmare
2. http://www.marketplace.org/topics/life/joplin-residents-carry
   -after-tornado

4. The Eat, Pray, Love Thing

1. http://www.cosmopolitan.com/career/interviews/a29085/jill
   -abramson-not-ashamed-of-getting-fired

5. What's Stopping You?

1. http://www.caltech.edu/content/neuroeconomists-confirm
   -warren-buffetts-wisdom
2. http://oregonhumanities.org/magazine/me-spring-2014/trapped-in
   -the-spotlight-courtenay-hameister/570

7. The Grind

1. http://www.raptitude.com/2010/07/your-lifestyle-has-already
   -been-designed

8. Money Money Money

1. http://www.wisebread.com
2. http://www.nytimes.com/2013/03/10/opinion/sunday/living-with
   -less-a-lot-less.html?pagewanted=all&_r=2&
3. http://link.springer.com/article/10.1007%2Fs12232-010-0093-6
4. http://bigthink.com/Mind-Matters/study-a-little-forethought-can
   -cure-the-urge-toward-mindless-accumulation

9. The Kids Will Probably Be All Right

1. http://www.reuters.com/article/2013/08/27/us-usa-families
   -idUSBRE97Q0TJ20130827; http://www.census.gov/hhes/families
2. http://usatoday30.usatoday.com/news/nation/census/2011-06-03
   -fewer-children-census-suburbs_n.htm
3. http://www.imdb.com/name/nm0911264

10. Not All Peaches and Cream

1. http://www.salon.com/2014/09/01/i_never_should_have_followed
   _my_dreams

12. Redefining Success and Work

1. http://www.marketplace.org/topics/world/our-lovehate
   -relationship-work

ACKNOWLEDGMENTS

First, my hand to my heart in thanks to the nearly three thousand attendees of the 2013 World Domination Summit who listened and lifted me up as I shared my story from the stage of the Arlene Schnitzer Concert Hall in Portland, Oregon. Your response that July morning is the inspiration for these pages, and you are all here in my bathtub full of kittens.

J. D. Roth is the reason I gave that speech. He asked me to do it. I said no, I'm not going to talk about one of the most difficult periods of my life in front of thousands of strangers, because that is not my idea of a good time. He said, "That's exactly why you should do it." I will never be able to fully express the gratitude I feel for his confidence in me and in my story. Thanks to Chris Guillebeau, the founder of WDS, for saying yes when J.D. suggested me as a speaker and for not panicking when I still had no idea, two weeks before the event, what I was going to say onstage.

To the eighty-plus of you who agreed to share your leap stories with me for this book: I couldn't include all of you, much as I wanted to! But please know that you *all* contributed to what I learned and ultimately shared here. This is your book, too.

Rick Horgan sent me an e-mail the night of the speech in which he wrote, "I'm Chris Guillebeau's editor at Random House. I was in the audience this morning, and I keep seeing a book title: *What the Hell Do I Do Now?*" Eleven days later we had a deal. Eleven days! The book title changed, and along the way our editing relationship was cut lamentably short, but I credit Rick with, and thank him for, seeing my potential as an author, not just a radio voice.

Eric Nelson called after I left *Marketplace* to see if I wanted to write a book about personal finance. Uh ... no. But he became my literary agent in those interim eleven days between speech and book deal and helped keep me on track. Deepest gratitude to Susan Rabiner for stepping in when Eric left for a new opportunity.

Leah Miller joined the team about a year into the process and proved to be a formidable manuscript editor. Thank you for understanding what I did and did not want this book to be, and for helping to shape it for the better. Diana Baroni picked up the ball after Leah's departure, and I'm grateful to her for making sure we got it over the goal line. Thank you to Penguin Random House for making me a published author.

I've been blessed with talented and generous colleagues over my twenty-plus-year career. Tom Goldman gave me my start in public radio. Henry Sessions was an early radio role model, and I couldn't have asked for a better TV co-anchor and friend than Jim Leinfelder. David Greene signed me to the team at *Only a Game* in Boston, joining Gary Waleik and my eventual maid-of-honor Katy Clark, and Bill Littlefield, who was and always will be the writer I strive to emulate without any real hope of doing so. There is no more talented radio editor on the planet than (Uncle) Ken Bader, who polished my prose in the WBUR newsroom, and Lisa Mullins is the consummate friend and radio host who to this day schools the rest of us in How It's Done. And while I was off the radio track for a couple of years, Norman Birnbach proved that being a good boss and a good friend don't have to be mutually exclusive.

I will always be grateful to J. J. Yore and Jim Russell for hiring me in 2001 to host the *Marketplace Morning Report*, the start of eleven years inside the newsroom where I so desperately wanted to work from the outset of my career. That shop gave me access to extraordinary colleagues for more than a decade, none more so than Paddy Hirsch, who served as the senior producer of *Marketplace Money* in my final year there. I wish we could have taken the show where we wanted it to go and where it deserved to go, but, instead, as my friend, Paddy gave me the confidence and strength to leave a place that was no longer good for me. He believed in my new future before I did.

To my *Marketplace* listeners: I miss you dearly and hope you're continuing to save more than you spend!

Teachers are everything in this world, and I am lucky to count among those who inspired me deeply: Bob Hamm, John Welty, the late Candy (Noyes) Morrison, Pat Lotz, and Dorothy Fahlman.

So many friends have contributed to this effort just by being there for me and engaging in heartfelt and helpful discussions about the Big Questions: Mia Dunn, Candice Rogers, Karen McManus, Sean and Diana Egusa, Matt and Nicole Janssen, Adam McIsaac (who also, let history show, sent the tweet that inspired the speech), Nat Katz, Heidi Moore, Liz Weston,

Steve Chiotakis, Deb and Fabricio Lopez, Karen Kiefaber, Elizabeth Babor, and Julie Campoy. You may not have realized it at the time, but your counsel—over coffee, lunch, drinks, dinner, trips to Santa Barbara wine country—made it possible for me to get my thoughts straight on what this book should really be about. And a giant bear hug to Bill and Nina Graham for providing a quiet space at Mammoth Lakes for me to think and write during this process.

My parents, to whom this book is dedicated, are the best a girl could ever hope for, and I cannot believe how fortunate I am that fate picked them for me. I love you more than I can possibly express, and I hope in these pages you find the gratitude I feel for being your daughter. Please take every bit of the credit for anything that is good and honorable about me.

And finally, to Dan: for not flinching that day in August 2012 when you came home to find me curled up in a ball in the backyard, sobbing that "I have to quit." You never once questioned my decision or my ability to rebound from a deep sense of despair, betrayal, and fear. You have provided unyielding support for me and for my career throughout our relationship. For all of that, and so much more, thank you.